The Revelation of Restoration

By
Dr. Ben Attah

Copyright © 2000, 2012 by Dr. Ben Attah

The Revelation of Restoration
by Dr. Ben Attah

Printed in the United States of America

ISBN 9781624199868

All rights reserved solely by the author. The author guarantees all contents are original and do not infringe upon the legal rights of any other person or work. No part of this book may be reproduced in any form without the permission of the author. The views expressed in this book are not necessarily those of the publisher.

Unless otherwise indicated, Bible quotations are taken from The King James Version of the Bible.

www.xulonpress.com

PARTNER WITH US

You can be of help to us! Beloved, you can support any of the activities we are doing to expand the kingdom of God. If this book has blessed your life and if you have been delivered through the guidance of this book; you can help us spread the good tidings.

You can be of help in the following ways:

➢ **Tithes, Vows, Seed Faith and Offerings** – You can pay your Tithes, Vows, Seed Faith or Offerings through any of the banks in Nigeria as listed below:

o **Zenith Bank PLC, Ogudu GRA Branch, Lagos** – account number 1011053946
o **Ecobank Nigeria PLC, Motorway Alausa, Ikeja, Lagos- account number 0007152448**
o **Access Bank PLC, Allen Branch, Ikeja, Lagos – account number – 0103522541**
o **Skye Bank PLC, Isheri Branch, Lagos** – account number 1771146440

➢ **Book Ministry** – God has helped his servant to write some very inspiring books with deep insights. About 97 of these books are presently unpublished. You can partner with us in this area. Please call +234- 802-640-2441 or +234-818-207-5453 or send a mail to : attahben@rocketmail.com or newlightcovenant@ymail.com

➢ **Church Planting Program:** You can partner with us in the area of Church planting. Our ministry has a global mandate to take the gospel to the entire world. In order to fulfill this mandate we are training pastors and posting them out to branches. You can support the work by donating lands, houses, warehouses, vehicles, musical equipment or money toward this purpose as the Spirit of God will lead you. Please call +234- 802-640-2441 or +234-818-207-5453 or send a mail to : attahben@rocketmail.com or newlightcovenant@ymail.com

Gospel Sponsors: You can sponsor or contribute to any of our programs e.g. Radio and Television broadcasts, Crusades, Serminars, outreaches, Schools etc. your efforts and inputs shall be appreciated and God would graciously reward. Please call +234- 802-640-2441, +234-806-6286016 or +234-818-207-5453 or send a mail to : :attahben@rocketmail.com or newlightcovenant@ymail.com

➤ **BE IN TOUCH**

For further spiritual assistance, prayers, deliverance or counseling or preaching or teaching engagements etc; please contact the author at any of the following addresses:

New Light Covenant Church
a.k.a. The millionaires' Church

Office Address: 16-18 Wilmer Street, Isheri, Off Ojodu-Berger Bus stop, Lagos, Nigeria

Postal Address: P.O. Box 8259, Ikeja, Lagos, Nigeria

Website: http://www.newlightcovenntchurch.org/
Email: attahben@rocketmail.com
Or: newlightcovenant@ymail.com

Telephone: +234- 802-640-2441 or +234-818-207-5453
　　　　　　+234-806-6286016

PRAYER REQUESTS

Please send your prayer requests to us through the addresses above. Also, feel free to visit us. Our ministry prayer warriors will raise a prayer covering over you, your family, business etc for God's blessing, divine health, breakthroughs as you support the work of God in our hands. God bless you!

Contact Address:
Dr. Ben Attah
New Light Covenant Church
16/18 Wilmer Street, Isheri
Off Ojodu/Berger Bus Stop, Lagos
Postal Address: P.O. Box 8259, Ikeja, Lagos, Nigeria
Website: http://www.newlightcovenntchurch.org/
Email: attahben@rocketmail.com
Or: newlightcovenant@ymail.com
Telephone: +234- 802-640-2441 or +234-818-207-5453
+234-806-6286016

The Revelation of Restoration

*"If they obey and serve him,
they shall spend their days in prosperity
and their years in pleasures.
But if they obey not,
they shall perish by the sword,
and they shall die without knowledge'.
Job 36: 11-12*

TABLE OF CONTENT

Dedication... v

Foreword... vi

Preface.. viii

Chapter One: The Introduction to the Book of Job........................... 1

Chapter Two: Job's Personality: Righteousness with Prosperity....... 10

Chapter Three: Satan is always around.. 23

Chapter Four: Influences of environment on man........................... 35

Chapter Five: What we say matters.. 46

Chapter Six: The need for an intermediary...................................... 56

Chapter Seven: Wealth and poverty - The sharp contrast................. 66

Chapter Eight: The Restoration of Man... 76

Chapter Nine: The Great Questions... 84

Chapter Ten: Hypocrisy - The greatest Sin...................................... 97

Chapter Eleven: Conclusion... 109

DEDICATION

This book is dedicated to Late Mr. Ekpenyong Attah (my earthly father) who during his life time made so many references to Job as the suffering man of the Bible. My father lived and died without really understanding the mystery of the book of Job.

His frequent reference to the book of Job later provoked my intense study of this book of the Bible. This work is a product of inquisition, study and revelation. It is intended to unveil the promises of God as revealed to Job.

FOREWORD

*V*ery few men or women with outstanding success in their secular profession are committed to the Ministry of the Word and also loyal in their local churches. Dr. Ben Attah is one. With confidence as his present pastor, I have cause to assert that he has a productive faith.

There is no joy like the thrill of walking in the exact knowledge of God's word. This is not knowledge based on the physical senses, but on the revealed word of God. This became Job's greatest discovery.

At the end of his period of trial, he declared:

> *"I have heard of thee by the hearing*
> *of the ear; but now mine eye seeth thee.*
> *And the Lord turned the captivity of Job..."*
> *Job 42: 5,10a*

This book reveals much of the principles required for your restorative experience. In as much as before the catching away of the saints, there will be prophetic restoration of prosperity to the church. It is about the discovery of your hidden treasures in Christ in the last days.

TABLE OF CONTENT

Dedication..v

Foreword... vi

Preface.. viii

Chapter One: The Introduction to the Book of Job............. 1

Chapter Two: Job's Personality: Righteousness with Prosperity....... 10

Chapter Three: Satan is always around............................. 23

Chapter Four: Influences of environment on man............ 35

Chapter Five: What we say matters.................................. 46

Chapter Six: The need for an intermediary...................... 56

Chapter Seven: Wealth and poverty - The sharp contrast............. 66

Chapter Eight: The Restoration of Man............................ 76

Chapter Nine: The Great Questions................................. 84

Chapter Ten: Hypocrisy - The greatest Sin...................... 97

Chapter Eleven: Conclusion..109

PREFACE

As a child, we were never allowed to open to the book of Job in the Bible. This was often referred to as the book of suffering. My late father Mr. Ekpenyong Attah often referred to himself as Job anytime calamity befell him. Unlike the Job of the Bible, he died prematurely.

Even after the death of my earthly father, I had always been scared of referring to the book of Job. In 1994, God specifically told me to study the book of Job and deliver myself from the fear of the book. God later told me in 1996 to write a book with the truth of the scripture. The primary vision of writing this book was inspired by my Pastor and Bishop Late Hafford Ilupotaife (Faith Revival Ministries Lagos, Nigeria). He showed keen interest in the subject.

To my greatest amazement, my discovery in the book of Job was contrary to my preconceived notion. I discovered that all the calamities of Job lasted for only 9 months and not a lifetime. I also discovered that Job was 70 years old when calamities befell him, and he lived 140 years after the calamities in prosperity and pleasures!

This book is a discovery of a lifetime. The book of Job is a complete threatise of God's relationship with man. The book relates man's inability to understand the supremacy of God. There are wonderful lessons to learn. The gap between the reasoning of ordinary man and the actions of the Almighty

God; the exploits/techniques of Satan is exposed. The strength of the power of the tongue displayed. The requirement for deliverance exposed. The precept that confession must be made before forgiveness is valid. There is a lot to learn.

After Job's restoration, even his enemies gave gifts to him. The restoration power of the Most High God is manifested. God is our justifier. No man can be righteous of his own accord.

The book closes with the message of Jesus Christ the mediator between God and man. A comparison is made between the first and the second Adam. The conclusion of the book is that man could be righteous if he depends on God. God is seen as the justifier not man, the key thing being that Job was justified by God. Justification is only in presence of God. In the New Testament, the blood of Jesus justifies us.

Welcome to the adventure of revelation that must usher you into the sanctuary of restoration and get you better equipped for exploits in life. Your life must wear a new look by the time the Lord is through with you in this encounter.

CHAPTER 1

INTRODUCTION TO THE BOOK OF JOB

*T*he book of Job is the 18th book of the Bible. The book has 42 chapters, 1070 verses, and 10,102 words. There is very little prophecy in the book: it has only one verse of fulfilled prophecy and three verses of unfulfilled prophecies. This book is of spectacular interest having the drama of life in print. The book highlights the difference between the thoughts of God and that of man. The book of Prophet Isaiah summarizes the gap between God and man's

> *"For as the rain cometh down, and the snow from heaven, and returneth not thither, but watereth the earth, and maketh it bring forth and bud, that it may give seed to the sower, and bread to the eater:*
>
> *So shall my word be that goeth forth out of my mouth: it shall not return unto me void, but it shall accomplish that which I please, and it shall prosper in the thing whereto I said it".*
> *Isaiah 55:10-11*

God has clearly declared through the mouth of the prophet that his ways are higher, better and organized way.

> *"For my thoughts are not your thoughts, neither are your ways my ways, saith the Lord. For as the heavens are higher than the earth, so are my ways higher than your ways, and my thoughts than your thoughts'.*
> *Isaiah 55: 8-9*

This point is clearly made in the book.

Author(s): Who wrote the book of Job? This may not really be what believers are interested in. For the sake of interest, we can state the following:

- The main part of the book appears to have been written by one person using the free flow of literature and linguistics.

- Bible scholars believed that the book was written by Job before the giving of the law by Moses, the ending portion giving statistics about what was written by Moses. There are some proofs to this. Moses could have done this during his 40 years in the desert before God's call.

- The author of the book received a special revelation from God concerning the scenes/arrangements of heavenly protocols and discussions between Satan and God.

- The author was specially inspired by the Holy Spirit (2 Tim. 3:16) to record the conversation between Job, his friends, God and Elihu.

- The writer must have been an Israelite as all the other Old Testament authors, because through Israel came the revelation of God (Rom. 3:2)

- The book was written before the Law of Moses. There is no slight reference to the law throughout the book.

- Job and Moses lived at the same time in the vast wilderness (from Arabia Petra to the Persian Gulf). For 40 years, Moses was in that part of the country caring for Jethro's flock. Moses could have interacted with Job and accepted his writing for the Hebrews before God's call for exodus (departure/movement.)

- The poetry and writing style from Chapters 1 42:6 do not resemble Moses style of writing. Moses could have written the conclusion in Chapter 42: 7-end.

- Moses actually received a lot of revelations from God concerning so many things which he wrote about. He could have received the revelation of Job in any case.

- We can say that regardless of who wrote the book, it is highly inspired by God.

- The art of writing of books is not new. Job has on some occasions desired that his sufferings be documented into books:

  "Oh that my words were now written!
  Oh that they were printed in a book!
  That they were graven with an iron
  pen and lead in the rock for ever".
  Job 19: 23-24

- We see that the book was written and we can all use it for study and inspiration today. (see also Job 31:35)

- Job lived 140 years after his affliction. He was 70 years when afflictions came. The afflictions lasted for 9 months. It is possible that Moses lived into the time of Job during his experience in Jethro's house.

- If the book of Job were the original work of Moses, he would have placed it after the book of Genesis. The story in the book of Job happened before exodus, the Law, etc. The style in Job 42: 7-17 was in agreement with the style of writing in the Pentateuch (Moses' books).

- God being displayed as the justification for humanity long before Jesus came on the scene.

Job's Genealogy

The Bible introduces Job as a man in the land of Uz. (Job 1:1). The land of Uz was located according to the Old Testament map South of Edom and West of Arabia, extending to the borders of the Chaldeans. It is possible that the land of Uz could have comprised of Arabia-Petra (Lam. 4:21; Jer. 25:20).

The name Job actually means afflicted. This is why modern Christianity teaches that we should not bear all such foolish names. In our part of the world, some people are called "Ekpo" (translated as Ghost) or "Ekpe" (Lion). It could be that the name attracted Satan to bring affliction his way. You must be careful with the names you give to your children.

Job was an Israelite. Do not be surprised. He was actually the third son of Issachar, the son of Jacob (Gen. 46:13, Ezekiel 14:14, 20). We shall discuss his personality in the next chapter. Job was a small boy when his father Issachar accompanied his grandfather Jacob to the land of Egypt. How Job left Egypt for Uz is what we are not told. The truth is that all the Israelites did not just stay put in Egypt. Moses also departed Egypt for the Median desert.

Purpose of the Book

The main purpose of the book of Job is to give light concerning human sufferings, calamities, sickness, diseases, pain and other vices which could be interpreted differently by different people. The book identifies Satan as the midwife of all problems that befalls man. The book of Job records that the thoughts of man, conversion, and obedience to God's word can establish him.

God is represented here as a justifier and deliverer when his people call upon him for help. A lot of truths are exposed here:

- A righteous man cannot be tempted beyond what God allows. The devil could not kill Job.

- The devil cannot bring trouble your way unless God permits him.

- God will only allow the devil to test us when he knows that we can pass the test.

- Sin, hypocrisy, and fear are the seed Satan will sow in us to enable him penetrate us.

- The effects of suffering on a man of God.

- The role of human friends in times of trials.

- The sweetness of the end being better than the beginning.

Not only Job, some Israelites departed to Edom and other neighbouring localities after the fierce phase of famine. No wonder then the Bible talks about the children of Issachar:

> *"And of the children of Issachar, which were men that had understanding of the times to know that Israel ought to do;..."*
> *1 Chronicles 12:32*

In the analysis of the different tribes of Israel during the exploits of David as king of Israel, it could be noticed that only 200 men of Isaachar origin went to Ziklag as against at least 3000 supplied by other tribes. This buttresses the fact that Job and a few of his brothers had left Egypt long before the Exodus.

Job was a Jew living in a gentile country. In the Old Testament, the Jews exhibited the advantage of the Abrahamic covenant:
East is normally used to refer to Edom, Media, Persia, Assyria, Mesopotamia, Amalek, etc or the neighbourhood

> *"What advantage then hath the Jew? or what profit is there in circumcision? Much every way: chiefly because that unto them were committed the oracles of God"*
> *Romans 3: 1-2*

Bible Doctrines in the Book

Evil comes from the devil. Every good gift comes from God. Job was a very religious man as it was understood and practiced in his time. He only knew of the traditions and revelation up to his time, being a grandson of Jacob. He was born about 352 years after Noah died, about 200 years after Shem died.

Shem lived 602 years after the flood (Genesis 11: 10-11). This agrees with the year Abraham left for Canaan (75 years old). Isaac was sixty years old when he had Jacob (Genesis 25:26). Jacob was about 85 years old when Issachar was born. Issachar was 30 years old when affliction came. Bible Scholars based on this calculation believe that this would be 772 years after the flood.

The Language in the Book

The language is different from what is found in other books of the Bible. The language of Job is predominantly poetic. The logical use of words is predominant. The wisdom of God in creation, its creatures and features displayed are a beauty to diagnose.

Anthropomorphism - the ascription of human bodily parts, attribute and passions to God and taking the substantiating statements of scripture literal is very predominant. In the area where God comes on the scene in the book of Job, it is true that the discourses were very frank irrespective of the parties involved.

In this book, we shall look at all the different aspects of the book of Job and how we as Christians can rise unto the occasion. The major characters in the book only 8 of them Job, his wife, his three friends (Eliphaz, Bildad and Zophar), Elihu and God make it easy to follow the story.

In the subsequent chapters, we shall be able to take the lessons from this book.

CHAPTER 2

JOB'S PERSONALITY:
Righteousness with Prosperity

Righteousness with prosperity! This could easily be used to describe the man - Job. There is no other way of describing him. In those days, we believed that it was impossible to be prosperous and righteous at the same time. Long before the law was given, Abraham was very rich, his great-grand son Job, was also very rich.

His Location:

Job stayed in a town called Uz. This was the town founded by Huz, Nahors (Abraham's brothers) son. (Gen. 22:20-21) In those days, most villages were named after their founders. The promise of God is to prosper you irrespective of your location.

> *"For I know the thoughts that I think*
> *Toward you, saith the Lord,*
> *thoughts of peace, and not of evil,*
> *to give you an expected end".*
> *Jeremiah 29:11*

If Job could prosper in an unknown village, then you do not need a visa to America before prosperity would catch up with you. Once a man begins to prosper, his prosperity would define his location.

Job's Righteousness

This is how the Bible introduces Job:

"There was a man in the land of Uz, whose name was Job; and that man was perfect and upright, and one that feared God, and eschewed evil".
Job 1:1

Job's righteousness was not a hidden one. The Almighty God recognized, admired his righteousness and even testified of him saying:

"... Hast thou considered my servant Job, that there is none like him in the earth, a perfect and an upright man, one that feareth God, and escheweth evil?"
Job 1:8 (Job 2:3)

Wow! You can see God calling man perfect. Can He also call you perfect? There are four words used to describe Job's piety here.

1. *Perfect*

    The word perfect is used to describe Job. This connotes complete simplicity, sincerity, being free from all types of guile. The Hebrew word translated perfect here is ***tam***. This word is also translated plain (Gen. 25:27); Upright (Prov. 29:10); and Undefiled (Songs of Solomon 5:2; 6:9). It also means being free from any form of evil intention towards any man, or any tendencies of evil.

2. *Upright*

The root Hebrew word ***vashar*** is translated upright. It is also translated right (Ex. 15:26); righteous (Job 4:7; 23:7); Just (Prov. 29:10); Straight (Jer. 31:9) and Equity (Mic. 3:9). Job was seen to be upright even in the sight of God.

3. *Feared God:*

To have deep respect for (reverential fear). The root Hebrew word here is ***vare***. The fear of God is what many believers lack today. Job had it up to the point that God testified about it in his life.

4. *Eschewed Evil:*

This means to decline, depart from, pluck away, avoid, withdraw or be sour against evil. This does not mean that he did not have opportunities to commit evil, but he deliberately refused to commit sin.

If Job could live above sin even when Jesus had not yet shed his blood as atonement for sin, then you can equally live above sin by the power of Christ. Righteousness is a necessity for prosperity. Anybody can be rich today and poor tomorrow. God's own prosperity endures forever. This endurance of prosperity is on the ticket of righteousness.

"Righteousness exalteth a nation:
but sin is a reproach to any people.
Proverbs 14:34

Job's Prosperity:

The Bible writes about Job:

"And there was born unto him seven sons
and three daughters.
His substance also was seven thousand sheep,
and three thousand camels and five hundred
yoke of oxen, and five hundred she asses,
and a very great household; so that this man
was the greatest of all the men of the east".
Job 1:2-3

"So the Lord blessed the latter end of Job
more than his beginning: for he had
fourteen thousand sheep, and six thousand camels,
and a thousand yoke of oxen, and a
Thousand she asses. He had also
Seven sons and three? Daughters".
Job 42: 12-13

The above record is only for the moving assets. There is no record of the amount of gold, silver, money stored up in the house. The quoted verses of Job 1:2-3 represents assets before the affliction while the record in Job 42: 12 represents the assets after the affliction. Job's restored wealth as far as moving assets (animals) were concerned, were a double of what he had before the affliction.

We shall try to put some values to these wealth so as to help us appreciate Job's disposition as a believer. After the restoration, he had:

(a) 14,000 sheep @ N5,000   = N70,000,000
(b) 6,000 camels @ N20,000   = N120,000,000
(c) 1,000 yokes of oxen is at least 2000 oxen
    2,000 oxen @ N35,000   = N70,000,000
(d) 1,000 asses @ N20,000   = N20,000,000
                                     ─────────────
                                     N280,000,000

This is N280m only (approximately $3m)

A man having $3m in moving assets cannot be a mean man. You can begin to imagine the houses, cars, employees required to keep and control these animals. Don't forget that this man was this rich about 5000 years ago.

Job knew a lot about silver and gold, he knew the secrets of getting them. He spoke to his friends about the silver and gold:

> *"Though he heap up silver as the dust,*
> *and prepare raiment as the clay;*
> *He may prepare it, but the just shall put it*
> *on, and the innocent shall divide the silver".*
> *Job 27:16-17*

In the days of Job and even today, riches is counted in silver and gold. The value of the animals shown above is just to help guide our imagination of the wealth of Job. God will prosper any man that is righteous in his sight. Believers should call the bluff; the wealth of God is for the righteous.

In order to do this, believers must understand the truth that:

➢ **God is wealthy:** Wealth, real wealth belongs to God. If we have this at the back of our minds then, it would not surprise us why Job feared God and was wealthy.

> *"Now therefore, if ye will obey my voice*
> *indeed, and keep my covenant, then ye shall*
> *be a peculiar treasure unto me above all*
> *people: for the earth is mine..." Exodus 19:5*

> *"The earth is the Lord's, and the fullness*
> *thereof: the world, and they that dwell*
> *therein".Psalms 24:1*

> *"The silver is mine and the gold is mine,*
> *saith the Lord of Hosts". Haggai 2:8*

> *"For every beast of the forest is mine, and*
> *the cattle upon a thousand hills".*
> *Psalms 50:10*

➤ **Wealth is a gift from God:** Goodness is one of the basic attributes of God. God gives good things. Prosperity is a gift from Him; therefore prosperity is good.

> *"But thou shalt remember the Lord*
> *thy God: for it is he that giveth thee*
> *power to get wealth,..."*
> *Deut. 8:18*

Your own wealth is just about to explode. Hold on to God, trust him to release your wealth. I prophesy to you that the hour for your financial explosion is now.

Why did God give Job so much wealth?
People that God trusts He gives them riches. Any man that God can testify about calling "upright", "blameless", such a man will enjoy riches from God. The level of your righteousness therefore determines the height of your prosperity. All truth is parallel. This is the measure, the meter of prosperity.

Abraham was upright and God prospered him.

> *"And Abram was very rich, in cattle,*
> *in silver, and in gold". Gen.13:2*

> *"And Abraham was old, and well stricken in age: and the Lord had blessed Abraham in all things"*
> *Gen. 24:1*

Abraham had **all things.** There was nothing lacking in his house. Of his son, Isaac, the Bible says:

> *"Then Isaac sowed in that land, and received in the same year an hundred fold: and the Lord blessed him. And the man waxed great, and went Forward, and grew until he became very great: For he had possession of flocks, possession of herds, and great store of servants:..."*
> *Gen. 26:12-14*

Abraham, Isaac, Jacob, Job prospered before the law was given to Moses. David, Solomon, etc. prospered after the law was given. From all these, it is seen that the yardstick for prosperity has been and will always be righteousness. For every man that puts his trust in God shall prosper for truly God is willing and able to prosper him.

Divine Security:
A Component of Godly Prosperity

God secured Job. Even Satan testified of the divine security which Job enjoyed:

> *"Hast not thou made an hedge about
> him and about his house, and about all
> that he hath on every side?
> Thou hast blessed the work of his hands,
> and his substance is increased in the land"*
> *Job 1:10*

Any man that is righteous will enjoy divine security. Job enjoyed divine security/protection.
The promise of God is that HE will watch over his own.

> *"He shall call upon me, and I will
> answer him: I will be with him in
> trouble; I will deliver him,
> and honor Him".* *Psalm 91:15*

> *"No weapon that is formed against thee shall
> prosper: and every tongue that shall rise against
> thee in judgement thou shall condemn.
> This is the heritage of the servants of the Lord, and their
> righteousness is of me, saith the Lord".* *Isaiah 54:17*

I know that we will all like to enjoy divine security. In the last scripture quoted, the Bible says it is "the heritage of the servants of the Lord" To enjoy divine protection/preservation, long life, security, etc., a man needs to be called "the servant of the Lord". All Job's friends knew him as "the servant of the Lord".
Are you a Christian? Do people know you as a Christian?

What is God's testimony about your righteousness or commitment to righteousness? I think the book of Job will reveal the deep things of God to us. Job's personality was an embodiment of righteousness, prosperity and security. When you walk with God, you will be rich, and apart from that, you will be secured. In our country today, security is a big problem. The promise of God is certain, you will be divinely secured. If Job was secured, you can be.

No wonder then God could tell Satan about Job. He was proud of Job's personality.

> *"And the Lord said unto Satan,*
> *Hast thou considered my servant Job,*
> *that there is none like him in the earth,*
> *a perfect and an upright man, one that*
> *feareth God, and escheweth evil?"*
> *Job 1:8*

> *"Let them shout for joy, and be glad*
> *that favour my righteous cause: year, let*
> *them say continually, let the Lord be*
> *magnified which hath pleasure in the*
> *prosperity of his servant".*
> *Psalm 35:27*

In all cases God is looking for servants, faithful men and women that God could be proud of. God wants to rejoice in your breakthroughs, He wants to tell Satan about your success. Receive it now in the name of Jesus!

Blessing to Others: An Attribute of Job's Nature

Job was not only rich, his riches reached out to many people. Job said of himself:

> *"Because I delivered the poor that cried, and the fatherless, and him that had none to help him ...*
> *I was eyes to the blind, and feet was I to the lame. I was a father to the poor:..."*
> *Job 29:12-16*

The man Job was many things to many people. In the scripture quoted above:

(a) He delivered the poor
(b) He delivered the fatherless
(c) He delivered the homeless
(d) He blessed those who were ready to perish
(e) He caused the widows heart to sing for joy
(f) He defended the cause of the need
(g) He was eyes to the blind
(h) He was feet to the lame
(i) He was father to the poor
(j) He broke the jaws of the wicked

The purpose of God's blessing is that we might be a blessing to others. God told our father Abraham:

> *"And I will make of thee a great nation, and I will bless thee, and make thy name great; and thou shalt be a blessing".*
> *Gen.12:2*

Paul admonishes the Galatians Church.

> *"As we have therefore opportunity, let us do good unto all men, especially unto them who are of the household of Faith". Gal. 6:10*

Job's personality was enviable, his integrity was unsurpassed and was rich. He was righteous before God, he was a blessing to humanity, He was a threat to the devil and God gave him absolute security. His trials and the testing of his faith were only for 9 months out of the 211 years which he lived the earth. Do you still think that Job was a suffering man?

Job is an example of a man that has conquered the forces of nature by operating a higher law. He had a kind and tender heart, the poor and the needy benefited from his scholarship programs. He was a blessing to many. Job was a total man. God is speaking to you to be like the man Job. If only you can be righteous, you can prosper. If you can be faithful to God, you can prosper and enjoy divine protection. If you can reach out to humanity, God will open a book of remembrance for you and will account it for righteousness.

Believer, let us arise and accept the simplicity of the gospel. God is looking for men who would depend on him; who would be faithful to him. Can He count on you?

CHAPTER 3

SATAN IS ALWAYS AROUND

We see the devil Satan displayed in the book of Job. A lot of references were made to Satan in the seeming misfortune of Job. The archenemy of God and man is mentioned here by his name. He is not even mentioned by name in the book of Genesis. It is clear in Genesis 3 that there was an invisible enemy who caused the fall of Adam, even though he is shown as using the body of the serpent.

Satan is not an error of the mortal mind, neither is he a disease or germ as many think. Satan is not a being with hoofs nor an evil principle. In this chapter, we shall tell you a few things about Satan to enable you position yourself to defeat him always.

The Origin of Satan

Jesus Christ created Satan along with other beings, principalities and powers in heaven and on earth.

> *"All things were made by him; and without him was not any thing made that was made".*
> *John 1:3*

> *"For by him were all things created, that are in heaven, and that are in earth,*

> *visible and invisible,*
> *whether they be thrones, or dominions or*
> *principalities, or powers: all things were*
> *created by him, and for him; And He is*
> *before all things, and by him all things consist"*
> *Colossians 1:16-17*

> *"... beginning of the world hath been hid in God,*
> *who created all things by Jesus Christ"*
> *Ephesians 3:9*

> *"Where wast thou when I laid the foundations*
> *Of the earth? declare, if thou hast understanding.*
> *Who hath laid the measures thereof ...?*
> *whereupon are the foundations thereof fastened...?*
> *Job 38: 4-6*

According to the scriptures (Isaiah 14:12-14; Jeremiah 4: 23-26; Ezekiel 28:11-17; Luke 10:18; 2nd Peter 3: 4-8), Satan (also called Lucifer) had a kingdom on earth long before the 6 days re-creation of Genesis 1:3; 2:25. Lucifer led an offensive (rebellion) into heaven and was defeated. Lucifer and his followers (one third of the host of heaven) were thrown down from heaven to the earth. In those days, the earth was cursed, and flood and darkness covered the earth (Gen. 1:2).

> *"How art thou fallen from heaven,*
> *O Lucifer, son of the morning!*
> *how are thou cut down to the ground,*
> *which didst weaken the nations!*

*For thou hast said in thine heart, I will ascend into heaven, I will exalt my throne above the stars of God:
I will sit also upon the mount of the congregation, in the sides of the North:*

*I will ascend above the heights of the clouds:
I will be like the Most High"
Isaiah 14:12-14*

"And he said unto them, I beheld Satan as lightning fall from heaven". Luke 10:18

Satan regained ruler ship over the earth due to Adam's sin; he therefore usurped man's dominion by plotting and executing his fall from glory. He became a dictator to man as long as man became his subjects. Each man can now by the power of the gospel defeat Satan, and rid him of this unnecessary relationship. The light of the glorious gospel is to set us free from all the works of Satan.

The Satanic Ministry

The Satanic Ministry is a negative one. No good thing can ever come from the devil. The fruits of his ministry are evil. The following will help you to understand the types of work Satan can do:

➢ He is the deceiver of all men.

> *"And the great dragon was cast out, that old serpent, called the devil, and Satan, <u>which deceiveth the whole world;</u> he was cast out into the earth...".*
> *Revelations 12:9*

➢ He tempts men. (Mark 1:13; 1 Cor. 7:5)

➢ He causes all sicknesses, diseases, physical and mental maladies. The case of Job is an example. (Acts 10:38)

➢ He is the leader of all sinners, backsliders, and rebels. (Matt. 9:34; Ephesians 6:10-18; 1 Tim.5:15)

➢ He provokes man to sin against God. Job's wife asked Job to curse God and die.

➢ He is a thief. He steals the word of God and every good thing from men. (Matt. 13:19; Luke 8:12)

➢ He hinders answers to prayers. (Daniel 10:12-21)

➢ He causes divisions, strife, deadness, weakness, doubt and unbelief (1 Cor. 3:1-3; 1 Peter 5:8)

This list could be elongated. This is just to give you an idea of what Satan can do and the escape route created by the work of redemption.

Satanic Names & Titles

The book of Job is the only book that calls Satan by his original name. It is also good for believers to know that the Bible uses different names and titles for Satan. All the names and titles are related to the works of satanic ministry. It is advisable to note that the following names/titles are used for Satan:

- Lucifer (Isaiah 14:12-14)
- Devil (Rev. 12:9)
- Belzeebub (Matt. 10:25; 12:24)
- Belial (2 Cor. 6:15)
- Adversary (1 Pet. 5:8-9)
- Dragon (Deut. 12:3-12; 13:1-4)
- Serpent (2 Cor. 11:3; Rev. 12:9)
- God of this world (2 Cor. 4:4)
- The prince of this world (John 12:31)
- Accuser of our brethren (Rev.12:10)
- Enemy (Matt. 13:39)
- Tempter (Matt. 4:3)
- The wicked one (Matt. 13:38)
- That wicked one (1 John 5:18)
- A murderer (John 8:44)
- A sower of discord (Matt. 13:39)

Satan's Characteristics

In the book of Job, we see Satan manifesting in the affairs of men. This makes it necessary to discuss the issue in order to expose some tricks of the enemy. Many believers are so afraid of Satan that they think that Satan has equal power with God. Some even believe that Satan is omnipresent; these are all lies. The book of Job displays Satan in the real nature of who he is and what he can do.

❖ **Satan is a real person.** How do we know this? He has personal names given to him as already highlighted above. The Bible gives us personal descriptions of Satan. In Job 1:6, we see that Satan can move from place to place therefore coming into the presence of God from time to time. (Job 1:6 and 2:1). He is not permanently staying in God's presence.

In all the places where Jesus confronted the Devil, he dealt with him as a real person. Jesus Christ taught that the Devil was a real person (Luke 10:18; Acts 10:38; Rev.12:7-12). To buttress the fact that Satan is a real person, we can see him in conversations (Job 1:6-12; 2:1-7); because Satan has a body, he can only be in a place at a time. He was not in God's presence continually, he usually visits.

❖ **Satan has a heart.** The devil has been seen with a body. Since he was an angel, then he has a body, soul and spirit. Satan appeared two times in the book of Job with a body. Satan could speak. Speech is of the heart. God left Job in Satan's power; power is of the heart. The devil is seen to express desires in God's presence. Desire is of the heart. Please note that the devil has no good desire towards any man. All the time his desire towards man is evil.

God will necessarily allow the devil before he can strike. God asked the devil two questions:

> *"Whence comest thou?*
> *"Hast thou considered my servant Job…"*
> *Job 1:7-10/2:2-3*

It was God that allowed Satan to take away/destroy all Job's possessions.

> *"And the Lord said unto Satan,*
> *Behold all that he hath is in thy power;*
> *only upon himself put not forth thy hand".*
> *Job 1:12*

It was God that later allowed Satan to inflict Job with sicknesses and sores.

> *"And the Lord said unto Satan,*
> *Behold, he is in thine hand: but*
> *save his life". Job 2:6*

In all the two incidences, Satan was given limited access. It is wrong for Christians to believe that Satan is in control of the Universe. He has only limited access at a time. He cannot and dare not exceed his bounds.

❖ **Satan is the accuser of the brethren.** Having established that Satan is the archenemy of both man and God, he still accuses the believers before God. He accused Job of serving

God because of his riches and the divine protection that he enjoyed. Satan's theory as stated in the book of Job is that no man serves God without personal material gains. Satan suggests that believers would curse God to his face without such personal/material benefits. He accused Job, he is also accusing you. We know that his accusation is false. There is victory for you in Jesus name!

Agents of Satan

Satan could come to us through any of the people or things around us. In the case of Jesus, the devil wanted to use Peter to convince him not to shed his blood. The devil used a serpent (one of the occupants of the garden of Eden) to tempt Eve. In the case of Samson, it was the harlot woman. David the king fell to the beautiful wife of Uriah. The devil uses money, people and anything we hold so dear to enter us. Many men have had their wives co-operate with the Devil an example is Job's wife who asked the husband to curse God and die.

"Then said his wife unto him,
Dost thou still retain thine integrity?
Curse God, and die"
Job 2:9

"My breath is strange to my wife, though
I entreated for the children's sake of mine
own body". Job 19:17

Satan could use anything or anybody around you. We need to be vigilant in this life. Job lost his animals, children, money and health. The Devil looks for what we love to destroy. The wisdom of Christ puts us above all the satanic devices and agents.

Tempting Times

The Devil is older than man on the earth. He tries to come tempting when man is weak and/or assuming. Here are some examples on times/moments the devil presents a temptation:

- When you are celebrating wining and dining. Job's children were in their joyous moments when the devil struck (Job 1:18)
- When you are at ease. The Bible in 1 Peter 5:8 admonishes us to be sober and vigilant.

> *"Be sober, be vigilant; because your adversary the devil, as a roaring lion walketh about, seeking whom he may devour". 1 Peter 5:8*

- The devil strike oftentimes when we are prayerless, careless, indifferent or unfaithful.

> *"Therefore, let us not sleep as do others; but let us watch and be sober".*
> *1 Thess. 5:6*

- When we are in doubt or afraid. Fear is the tool the

devil uses to enter into us. Job was afraid of loosing his money, children and wealth. He lost all.

"For the thing which I greatly feared is come upon me, and that which I was afraid of is come unto me".
Job 3:25

♦ When you are in sin.

"He that committeth sin is of thedevil: for the devil sinneth from the beginning..."
1 John 3:8(a)

As Christians, anytime we sin, we allow the devil to lord over us. If we trust God, he will keep us above sin.

Which Way Out?

We seem to have said so much about the devil in this chapter that you may be thinking whether or not man can still succeed. I want to assure you that irrespective of the activities of the devil, there is hope for man. The devil will come with diverse kinds of temptations, but man can escape them all. God is totally committed to the success of his children.

"There hath no temptation taken you but such as is common to man: but God is faithful, who will not suffer you to be tempted above that ye are able; but will with the temptation also make a way

> *to escape, that ye may be able to bear it."*
> *1 Cor. 10:13*
>
> *"...for the accuser of our brethren is cast down, which accused them before our God day and night".*
> *Rev. 12:10(b)*

From the foregoing, we realize that:

1. Satan still accuses the brethren before God day and night.
2. God requires your testimony to nail the devil in his schemes against you.
3. Temptation is not a sin. You could fall for it (like Eve) or overcome it (like Jesus).
4. Every temptation is common to man. There is no problem that is new to humanity. Solomon wrote "Nothing new under the sun".
5. No temptation is beyond man's ability to overcome it. There is always a way of escape.
6. God must permit Satan before he gains victory over the Christian.
7. Victory or failure in the face of temptation is the making of the person being tempted.

The scriptures cannot be broken. Jesus has made adequate provision for all the Christians to survive the devil's onslaught. The truth is that God is thinking well about us. He does not desire that we should see evil. The price for our safety, security, prosperity, health, etc. has been paid. One of my favourite scriptures is 1 John 5:4:

> *"For whatsoever is born of God*
> *overcometh the world:*
> *and this is the victory that overcometh the*
> *world, even our faith".*

Even though the devil has the ability to appear before God accusing the believer "day and night", we have what it takes to overcome him "day and night". Therefore, Overcomer, rejoice!

> *"Submit yourselves therefore to God*
> *Resist the devil, and he will flee from you*
> *Draw nigh to God, and he will draw nigh*
> *to you".*
> *James 4:7-8(a)*

CHAPTER 4

INFLUENCES OF ENVIRONMENT ON MAN

In this chapter, we will look into the friends Job had. Social sciences believe that there are three major ways that men are influenced. These are association, observation and teaching. Association is about your daily interactions with your friends. Observation is what you see others do (physically, on television, radio drama, etc.). Teaching is by direct training. Among all these, association has the greatest impact on the lives of men. Most children always grow up to be like their parents. This is a product of association.

The Natural Man

The natural man is wicked. The Bible talks about the heart of the natural man.

> *"The heart is deceitful above all things,*
> *and desperately wicked: who can know it?"*
> *Jeremiah 17:9*

Man without Christ is full of trouble. From the time that Adam sinned against God; man lost the ability to be righteous. In the light of the book of Job, we see the following truths:

❑ The natural man takes to sin as fish takes to water.

> *"How much more abominable and filthy is man,*
> *which drinketh iniquity like water?" Job 15:16*

> *"The Lord looked down from heaven upon the children of men, to see if there were any that did understand, and seek God. They are all gone aside, they are all together become filthy: there is none that doeth good, no not one". Psalm 14:2-3*

Nature does not make anybody righteous in God's sight.

- The Old Testament saints were not totally reliable. An example is David who committed adultery, murder and all related sins. Even Peter sinned against the gentiles (Gal. 2:11-21)

- Man without Christ is filthy.

> *"If thou, Lord, shouldest mark iniquities, O Lord, who shall stand?" Psalm 130:3*

Man cannot be justified by his works. He has a tendency to sin against the Creator; he cannot be justified by himself. He is therefore helpless without an external assistance.

Our Friends

The people we call friends affect our life style and major decisions in life. The Bible recognizes friends and the effect they can have on us.

> *"Blessed is the man that walketh
> not in the counsel of the ungodly, nor
> standeth in the way of sinners, nor sitteth
> in the seat of the scornful". Psalm 1:1*

The contrast between the godly and the ungodly is evident in their association. Our associates play a major role in our reaction and/or behaviour.

> *"Yea, ye overwhelm the fatherless, and ye
> dig a pit for your friend". Job 6:27*

> *"What man is like Job, who drinketh up
> scorning like water?*
>
> *Which goeth in Company with the
> workers of iniquity, and walketh with
> wicked men" Job 34: 7-8*

From here, we begin to see where some of Job's problems came from. Most of our friends love our money or what they can get from us.

Job's Friends:

We have discussed a bit about Job's wife. Here, we see Job's three friends. The three friends were Eliphaz the Tenamite, Bilhad the Shuhite and Zophar the Naamathite. They came to meet Job at the time of his calamity. Going through the book of Job studiously, I will like to introduce Job's friends.

Eliphaz: Eliphaz the Temanite - He is believed to be connected to Esau and Edom (Genesis 36:4; 1 Chronicles 1:35-36, 53). The Temanites were famous in their wisdom (Jeremiah 49:7). In all the arguments, Eliphaz's standpoint was based on human experience of the carnal man. He was the first to answer Job. All that he said occupies four chapters in the book (4, 5, 15 and 22).

Bildad the Shuhite: Perhaps a descendant of Shuah, the youngest son of Abraham by Keturah who settled East of Palestine. (Compare Genesis 25:2,6) Bildad's argument was from the standpoint of human tradition. He was the second to answer Job. The things he said are found in three chapters (8, 18 and 25).

Zophar the Naamathite: He was probably from Naamah on the southern frontier of Judah. He was the last of three friends to answer Job. His arrangement was based on the stand point of human merit. The record of what he said occupies two chapters 11 and 20.

The three friends came to meet Job in the time of his calamity. What was their mission? We are told in Job 2:11 that their 2-fold purpose was to mourn with Job and to comfort him. They accomplished the first purpose easily for they wept, mourned, tore their clothes, sprinkled dust upon their heads, spoke no word for seven days. What a great multiplication of sorrows! Did God take pleasure in this? Please read on.

In the second purpose of comforting Job, the friends failed woefully in the attainment of this. When Job opened his mouth and cursed the day of his birth and began to justify himself and accuse God, the friends made a tirade against him. This provoked Job further into doing many other foolish things. The friends succeeded in mourning but never succeeded in comforting him. They achieved the opposite.

Let us do a summary on the achievement of Job's friends in the face of his calamity:

- They initially wept for Job for seven days. They could not immediately recognize Job probably because his body was covered with boils.

> *"...they lifted up their voice and wept:*
> *and they rent every one his mantle,*
> *and sprinkled dust upon their*
> *heads towards heaven.*
> *So they sat down with him upon the*
> *ground seven days and seven nights,*
> *and none spake a word unto him: for*
> *they saw that his grief was very great".*
> *Job 2: 12-13*

Weeping does not move God. It is not a prayer but a multiplication of sorrow. Medical science believes that weeping, grief, mourning, wailing and gnashing of teeth for seven days could complicate the medical condition. Many people may have mourned with you, or mourned for you. Did they change anything for the better?

- ❖ The friends of Job proved to be of no help. Job acknowledged that they were of no help. There are many friends like these in the world today.

> *"Did I say bring unto me? Or, give a reward for me of your substance? ... ... And ye dig a pit for your friend". Job 6:22-27*

- ❖ Job called them "miserable comforters".

> *"I have heard many such things: miserable comforters art ye all". Job 16:2*

> *"But ye are forgers of lies, ye are all physicians of no value". Job 13:4*

The friends could not even acknowledge God's testimony of Job. Neither did they recognize the existence of Satan. They succeeded in provoking Job all along.

- ❖ His friends were his main accusers. Like we had earlier said, Satan entered into Job's friends and used them against Job. They challenged Job's righteousness and pronounced him a sinner. They declared that he was suffering for his sins.

> *"Can the rush grow up without mire?*
> *Can the flag grow without water?"*
> *Job 8:11*
>
> *"Is not thy wickedness great?*
> *And thy iniquities infinite? ...."*
> *Job 22: 5-7*

❖ God was angry with Job's friends.

> *"... after the Lord had spoken these words unto Job, the Lord said to Eliphaz the Temamite, my wrath is kindled against thee, and against the two friends: for ye have not spoken of me the thing that is right As my servant Job hath".*
> *Job 42:7*
>
> *"Behold, God will not cast away a perfect man, neither will he help the evil doers:..."*
> *Job 8:20-22*

If God was angry with them, it means that what they did was not good.

Job was misjudged! Even the High Court Judge makes mistakes since he judges based on facts available to him. Some innocent people have been sentenced to death for offences they did not commit. Many people have been misjudged by friends and relations, are you one of them?

Job was misunderstood! Due to the wild statements made by Job, his friends misunderstood him, to be at war with God. Many people are misunderstood. When you buy a new car, you may be misunderstood for display of wealth than having need for the basic functions of a car. Suspicions of deeds and misdeeds have caused serious misunderstanding(s) among friends. Friends that do not share in the same goals and aspirations would always have misunderstanding.

Job was mistaken! He was mistaken for a thief, a worm, a sinner, and a fool. His wife mistook him. His friends mistook him. The end justifies the means the end of Job was better.

Mistaken, misjudged and misunderstood, Job appealed to his friends:

> *"Have pity upon me, have pity upon me,*
> *O ye my friends; for the hand of God*
> *hath touched me*
> *Why do ye persecute me as God, and*
> *are not satisfied with my flesh?"*
> *Job 19: 21-22*

Job's appeal for pity did not yield any positive result. Instead, the friends became more hardened and harsh in their answers to Job. Zophar accused Job of wickedness (Job 20: 1-28); Eliphaz insisted that Job was a hypocrite and guilty of many sins (Job 22: 1-9). They classed him with the lowest species of men on the surface of the earth (Job 22: 12-30). Bildad argued that no man can be just and clean before God and that not even the stars are clean in the sight of God (Job 25: 1-6). All these made Job to be provoked against God. He made so may negative utterances he would not have made if not by the presence of his friends.

What type of friends do you keep? The Bible offers a clear guidance on this.

> *"A man that hath friends must shew himself friendly: and there is a friend that sticketh closer than a brother".*
> *Proverbs 18:24*

> *"To him that is afflicted pity should be shewed from his friend; but he forsaketh the fear of the Almighty".*
> *Job 6:14*

To maintain friends, you must always celebrate with them. Above all, it is difficult to have a man we trust. The Bible warns us not to trust in man.

> *"Give us help from trouble: for vain is the help of man".*
> *Psalm 108:12*

What is your Yardstick for choosing your Friends?

"Be ye not unequally yoked together with

> *unbelievers: for what fellowship hath righteousness with unrighteousness? and what communion hath light with Darkness?" 2 Cor. 6: 14*
>
> *"I am a companion of all them that fear thee, and of them that keep thy precepts".*
> *Psalm 119:63*

Your environment affects you. It is impossible to be dissociated from the lifestyle of your associates. Your close associates may give a clean expression of who you are. You can come over this by making Jesus Christ your best friend. He is the ever-present help. He is the friend that sticks closer than a brother. You may wish to talk to him now.

A man whose friends are all armed robbers is not innocent; the same goes for a girl whose friends are harlots. The decision is yours. You may wish to dissociate yourself from some of your present friends. You can call it quits. Friendship is not by force. If you are a student reading this book and all your friends are not doing well in school, dissociate yourself from all of them. Associate yourself with men, women, boys and girls who are models of who you will like to be.

It might also interest you to know that Job maintained his integrity until his friends arrived. He did not utter guile from his mouth. Even when the wife confronted him, he still praised God in adversity, but when his friends came, he started boasting, cursing and talking wild. Is this your case? The blood of Jesus is able to set you free from the bondage of association.

CHAPTER 5

WHAT WE SAY MATTERS

What we say matters! Whether we are doing fine or not, what we say matters. **In good times, at bad times, at all times, what we say matters.** I am happy that we have dealt with man's associates in the previous chapter. Most of the things we say depend on the environment where we find ourselves.

As Christians, we should be careful how we speak. God has given us two eyes, two nostrils, two hands, two legs, but one mouth. We should see and hear more than we talk. The man Job was a different entity. Out of the 42 chapters in the book of Job, Job spoke 20 chapters (47.6%) of the book. In the whole of chapters 1 and 2, Job did not mess up by word of speech, he kept his integrity, but between chapters 3 and 40, Job said so many things against himself, God, his friends, etc.

What the Bible says:

The Bible is very explicit on the subject of the use of tongue. Some of the Bible lessons concerning the use of the tongue include:

• Life and death is in the mouth.

> *"Death and life are in the power of the tongue: and they that love it*

> *shall eat the fruit thereof"*
> *Proverbs 18:21*

He that uses his mouth rightly shall eat the good fruit of life. Examples of death by the tongue include: The 10 spies with evil report (Numbers 14: 36-37); Doeg the Edomite (1 Samuel 22: 9-10); Sennacherib (2 Kings 18:28-35), etc.

- The mouth can bring healing to a man.

> *"He that speaketh truth*
> *showeth forth righteousness...*
> *There is he that speaketh like the*
> *Piercing of a sword:*
> *but the tongue of the wise is health"*
> *Proverbs 12: 17-18*

> *"I shall not die, but live, and*
> *declare the works of the Lord"*
> *Psalm 118: 17*

- Everything in the world was created as a result of the spoken word. God said all things to being.
(Reference: Gen. 1:3, 6, 9, 11, 14, 20, and 24, etc. all start with "And God said")

> *"In the beginning was the Word,*
> *and the Word was with God,*
> *and the Word was God".*
> *John 1:1*

- The tongue is so important that it provides the bearing for which the entire life depends.

    "Even so the tongue is a little member, and boasted great things. Behold, how great a matter a little fire kindleth". James 3:5

    The tongue is like the steering of a car and it determines in which direction the vehicle moves.

- The Bible advises that there is need to tame our tongues. No cunning, persuasion or influence of men can tame the tongue. Salvation alone can tame the tongue of man.

    "But the tongue can no man tame; it is an unruly evil, full of deadly poison" James 3:8

    "Whoso keepeth his mouth and his tongue keepeth his soul from troubles" Proverbs 21:23

- Every careless word will be accounted for. Be careful what you say with your mouth.

    "Thou art snared with the words of hy mouth, thou art taken with the words of thy mouth" Proverbs 6:2

    "But I say unto you, that every idle word that men shall speak, they shall

give account thereof in the day of judgement.

*For by thy words, thou shall be justified,
and by thy words, thou shall be condemned".
Matthew 12: 36-37*

- You have what you say.

  What you possess, the position you attain, is a product of your confession.

  *"... he shall have whatsoever he saith".
  Mark 11:23*

  *"... and with the mouth confession is
  made unto salvation" Romans 10:10*

Christians can call whatever they require for their salvation: health, wealth, money, houses, etc. He could call them with his mouth and he will have them. How does Job fall in here.

What did Job say?

After his friends visited him and mourned, wept and cried for seven days, Job opened his mouth and started talking. As it has been said before, Job is used to talking. He spoke almost 50% of the total volume of the book of the Bible named after him. We shall examine what Job said and how this determined his future. Here are some examples:

One: In Job Chapter 3, Job opened his mouth to speak:

  ❋ He cursed his birthday (Verses 1-10)

- ❊ He lamented his infancy (verses 11-14)
- ❊ He lamented his manhood (verses 20-26)
- ❊ He pitied himself
- ❊ He regretted about living
- ❊ He made a confession of his fears (verse 25)

Two: In Chapter 6, Job replied Eliphaz. In this Chapter:

- ❊ Job accuses God of being his enemy (verse 2-8)
- ❊ He lamented the heaviness of his grief and calamity (verse 2)
- ❊ He prayed for God to destroy him in his misery (verse 8-13)
- ❊ He reproves his friends for their deception and lack of understanding (verse 14-20)
- ❊ Job maintained his independence in misery (verse 22-23)
- ❊ He admonished his friends for their bitter words (verse 24-27)
- ❊ He appealed to his friends to have faith in him (verse 28-end)

Three: In Chapter Seven - The summary of Job's speech is as shown below:
- ✿ Job longs to die presented his twelve fold grief (verse 1-10)
- ✿ Job bitterly accuses God of injustice and ill-treatment (verse 11 end)
- ✿ Job complained bitterly about life.

- Job wanted an end to his life
- He justified himself.

In the three chapters we have cited here, we see Job saying many things against himself, God, his future, etc. He accuses God of unfair treatment and justified himself in God's presence. Job walked the earth at a time when the knowledge of God's word was limited. There were some basic fallacies, which must be straightened out before one can really appreciate Job's utterances.

Basic Fallacies:

There are two great mistakes made by Job. These were basically due to his misunderstanding of God and his principles.

1. Job claimed that God had taken away his riches.

> *"Naked came I out of my mother's womb,*
> *and naked shall I return thither: the Lord*
> *gave and the Lord hath taken away;*
> *Blessed be the name of the Lord".*
> *Job 1:21*

This was ignorance in display. Unfortunately, Job did not know better. Though the narration in the book is very clear that Satan took his riches away, he believed that it was God. Job believed that God was in-charge of everything and was responsible for everything.

Unfortunately, this verse of the scripture is what some 'orthodox' churches use for burial ceremonies. It is also used for self-consolation in times of calamities. There are a lot of verses like this in the book of Job.

2. The second fallacy is the question in Chapter 2 verse 10:

> *"What? Shall we receive good at the hand of God, and shall we not receive evil?..."*

Job was like many Christians today who think that sickness, disease, pain, frustration, poverty and nakedness come from God. The book is explicit in recording the exploits of Satan in this area. The exposition of these truths helps us to understand the reality of the new covenant. If Job had an understanding of these truths, his utterances and confessions would have been different.

God knows everything. He does not cause everything. Even though the devil requires his permission to tempt man; God is not a tempter. He always grants the devil limited access to tempt a Christian.

> *"Let no man say when he is tempted, I am tempted of God; for God cannot be tempted with evil, neither tempted he any man..."*
> *"Every good gift and every perfect gift is from above, and cometh down from the Father of lights, with*

Whom is no variableness, ..."
James 1:13-17

Job complained, murmured and even accused God. He did not stop there. He justified himself before God.

*"Teach me, and I will hold my tongue:
and cause me to understand wherein
I have erred" Job 6:24*

*"Surely I would speak to the Almighty,
and I desire to reason with God"
Job 13:3*

*"... the just upright man is laughed to scorn"
Job 12:4*

*"My face is foul with weeping, and on
my eyelids is the shadow of death;
Not for any injustice in mine hands:
also my prayer is pure"
Job 16:16-17*

Job's grief was heavy. His problem was much. Job's knowledge of God was limited. We can understand why his suffering lasted for nine months. He spoke it into existence.

*"So am I made to possess months of vanity, and wearisome
nights are appointed to me".
Job 7:3*

> *"O that I were in months past, as in the days*
> *When God preserved me" Job 29:2*

With his mouth, he determined his length of trial; the type of sickness (Job 6: 2-3); displayed his ignorance (Job 6:4-6; 7:20); and expressed his fears and anxieties (Job 3: 24-25; 6:7)

Since life and death are in the power of the tongue, you can use your mouth positively. We are in the age of knowledge. As you read this book, you must become one of the greatest men God is raising for the end time harvest. You need money to preach the gospel. Your health is your inheritance in God. ***Please say with me***:

- ☺ **I can never be poor!**
- ☺ **I can never be broke!**
- ☺ **I can never be sick!**
- ☺ **I am always on top!**
- ☺ **I came from above, then I am above all!**
- ☺ **I am a victor and not a victim!**
- ☺ **I am a winner and not a loser!**
- ☺ **I am above always never beneath!**

Do not forget that Job's healing and restoration did not come until his confession changed. You can change your destiny today by changing your confession.

> *"I know that thou canst do everything and*
> *that no thought can be with holden from*

> *Thee ...therefore have I uttered that I*
> *understood not; things too wonderful for*
> *Me, which I knew not.*
>
> *"... I have heard of thee by the*
> *hearing of the ear: but now my eyes*
> *Seeth thee. Wherefore, I abhor myself,*
> *and repent in dust and ashes".*
> *Job 42: 1-6*

This was all Job needed to say to restore his fellowship with God. Admit his shortcomings, repent and ask for forgiveness from God. God forgave him and restored him.

There is hope for you that are down. The sick and the seemingly hopeless, there is a lifting up.

> *"When men are cast down, then*
> *thou shall say There is a lifting up ..."*
> *Job 22:29*

God is our justifier. You can change your confession today and stand justified in God's sight. You may want to make Psalm 141:3 your prayer:

> *"Set a watch, O Lord before my mouth;*
> *Keep the door of my lips".*

CHAPTER 6

THE NEED FOR AN INTERMEDIARY

"For he is not a man, as I am, that I should answer him, and we should come together in judgement.
Neither is there any daysman betwixt us, that might lay his hand upon us both".
Job 9: 32-33

In the above passage, Job realized that there was a yawning gap between man and God; and requested for a mediator or an intermediary or a "daysman". By so doing, Job prophesied the necessity for a mediator between God and man. Jesus Christ was later to fulfil this role in the New Testament.

In the pre-Christ Israel, the "Daysman" in a case of dispute between two friends was expected to be a friend of both parties. The word "daysman" was called "yakach" in Hebrew. This word means to be right, to argue, to justify, to decide. It also means to convict, judge, maintain, plead, rebuke, umpire, referee, reason or mediate. Job sincerely needed a mediator to understand why things were happening the way they did.

A mediator is the middle person that brings reconciliation between two parties at enmity.

> *"For there is one God, and one mediator between God and men, the man Christ Jesus".*
> *1 Tim. 2:5*

> *"Now a mediator is not a mediator of one, but God is one".*
> *Gal. 3:20*

Bible scholars agree that wherever there was a problem between God and man, he required a daysman to mediate. All other "mediators" in the Old Testament were seen as "types". Abraham mediated in God's arrangement to destroy Sodom. Moses on many occasions mediated in God's plan to destroy Israel. In the book of Job, Elihu is seen as a type of a mediator. All the mediators/types in the Old Testament were a pointer to the coming mediator between God and men the man Jesus Christ.

Elihu as a type of "JESUS CHRIST"

The mediator in the book of Job has some resemblance with Jesus Christ. Let us look at the similarities.

❖ Elihu was filled with the spirit of God and so was Jesus.

> *"The spirit of God hath made me, and the breath of the Almighty hath given me life".*
> *Job 33:4*

> *"The spirit of the Lord is upon me ..."*
> *Luke 4:18*

❖ Elihu was human.

> *"... I also am formed out of the clay".*
> *Job 33:6*

Elihu was the descendant of Buz, the second son of Nahor (Abraham's brother). Elihu had heard several things that contradicted his religious beliefs. The Bible makes it clear that Jesus Christ was "made flesh and dwelt among men".

❖ Elihu claimed to be standing in God's stead like Jesus Christ is the advocate on high.

> *"Behold, I am according to thy wish in God's stead ..." Job 33:6*

> *"Suffer me a little, and I will shew thee that I have yet to speak on God's behalf". Job 36:2*

> *"... And if any man sin, we have an advocate with the Father, Jesus Christ the righteous". 1 John 2:1*

❖ Elihu emphasized the need for an interpreter, a messenger, and atonement and a ransom. Elihu claimed to be the missing link between God and Job.

Elihu believed that there are very few messengers of God, and he was one. The messengers are not always able to contact the character that God is dealing with.

In this case, Elihu the messenger was in touch with the main character God was dealing with Job. The messenger was to show the character how to enjoy healing and restoration from God.

> *"If there be a messenger with him, an interpreter, one among a thousand, to shew unto man his uprightness:*
> *Job 33:23*

Elihu is to show the uprightness of God. Such uprightness brings deliverance and healing. The ransom makes it possible for God to restore the sick to life. It was He who found a ransom deliverer, redeemer by price.

> *"Then he is gracious unto him, and saith, Deliver him from going down to the pit: I have found a ransom".*
> *Job 33:24*

> *"And not only so, ... Lord Jesus Christ, by whom we have now received the atonement"*
> *Romans 5:11*

While Elihu is the ransom in the book of Job, Jesus Christ is the ransom for the New Testament church.

☦   Elihu desired to justify Job.

> *"If thou hast anything to say, answer me:*
> *Speak for I desire to justify thee".*
> *Job 33:32*

> *"There is therefore now no condemnation*
> *to them which are in Christ Jesus ..."*
> *Romans 8:1*

Those who are in Christ are justified. They are free from condemnation and from the law of sin and death. These justified people enjoy life and peace; they also walk in the spirit.

❖ Elihu desired to teach Job wisdom.

> *"If not, hearken unto me; hold thy*
> *peace, and I shall teach thee wisdom".*
> *Job 33:33*

Any man that teaches another wisdom must be a better man. Jesus is the wisdom of God. The similarity here is very profound.

❖ Elihu was the only one that accused and reprimanded Job. Job did not defend himself before Elihu. Elihu revealed God's will and purpose. He told Job of his insensitivity to God's direction, leadings and visions. Elihu accused Job of indiscipline, ignorance, and insensitivity to the spirit of God, self-righteousness, hypocrisy, rebellion and strife. He also accused Job of having bad friends.

> *"For God speaketh once, yea twice,*
> *yet man perceiveth it not.*
> *In a dream, in a vision of the night,*
> *when deep sleep falleth upon me,*
> *in slumberings upon the bed..."*
> *Job 33: 14-15*

> *"For Job hath said, I am righteous:*
> *and God hath taken away my judgement".*
> *Job 34:5*

> *"What man is like Job, who drinketh*
> *up scorning like water?*
> *Which goeth in company with the*
> *workers of iniquity, and walked*
> *with wicked men".*
> *Job 34: 7-8*

Unlike Job's reaction when his friends spoke with him, this time around he did not answer a word. Consider other accusations against Job in Chapters 34:12; 34-35 and Chapter 35:2.

It is only a man without sin that could accuse another of sin without any counter accusation. Elihu was indeed a mediator. Consider the role of Jesus as he charges the Pharisees and the Sadducees.

✞　　Elihu did not lie.

> *"For truly my words shall not be false*
> *He that is perfect in knowledge is with thee"*
> *Job 36:4*

> *"Should I lie against my right?..."*
> *Job 34:6*

Elihu may have been truthful as a man, but Jesus is the truth.

> *"Jesus said unto him, I am the way,*
> *the truth, and the life ..."*
> *John 14:6*

❖　Elihu magnified God in his utterances.

> *"For he will not lay upon man more*
> *than right; that he should enter*
> *into judgement with God*
> *He shall break in pieces mighty*
> *men without numbers and set*
> *others in their stead".*
> *Job 34:23-24*

He magnified God and his works. It takes somebody who is godly to glorify and magnify God for good things.

> *"Behold, God is great, and we know*
> *him not, neither can the number*
> *of his years be searched out ..."*
> *Job 36: 26-33*

✞ God came on the scene after Elihu finished speaking. Jesus is the word of God and He was there in the beginning.

> *"For it pleased the Father*
> *that in him should all fullness dwell".*
> *Colossians 1:19*

The Ministry of JESUS

In the Ministry of Jesus Christ, "the author and the finisher of our faith", we see him as a ransom. It was on his blood that the substitutional works on the cross was completed. He shed his blood as a ransom payment for our justification. His blood completed the substitutional works. Those who were poor, Jesus took their poverty. Those who were sick, He took their sicknesses in exchange for health.

> *"For ye know the grace of our Lord*
> *Jesus Christ that, though he was rich,*
> *yet for your sakes, he became poor,*
> *that ye through his poverty might be rich".*
> *2 Cor. 8:9*

On the cross, Jesus took my place. I am sure he took your place too. Every curse of the law, he took them so that we should enjoy the blessing of Abraham.

Jesus is our conqueror. He defeated Satan, He made captivity captive and because he defeated Satan, we enjoy the victory. We are the ones enjoying the victory without fighting a battle. That is why the Bible says that we are more than conquerors.

> *"Nay in all these things we are more than conquerors through him that loved us".*
> *Romans 8:37*

Jesus Christ is our advocate. He pleads our case before the Father.

> *"My little children, these things write I unto you, that ye sin not. And if any man sin, we have an advocate with the Father, Jesus Christ the righteous".*
> *1 John 2:1*

Jesus is our daysman, the mediator between God and man.

> *"... to declare his righteousness for the remission of sins that are past ..."*
> *Romans 3: 24-27*

The blood of Jesus justifies every sinner. (Further reading Romans 3: 18-25; Galatians 2:21; 3:10; Job 34:31-32). Jesus is our intermediary, our daysman. He has done the complete work for us.

Restoration is Possible

The greatest achievement of Elihu was to prepare Job's heart to receive God. Immediately Job came to the point of receiving God, his restoration became imminent. Elihu being a man could talk to Job about humanity and brought him to the point of knowledge to hear from God.

God can restore any man. It is never too late. The essence of Jesus coming unto the scene was to bring man back to God. Job had deviated from the truth. He had accused God for his misfortunes. He thought that God was responsible for his calamities. Elihu taught him wisdom and brought him to the point of knowledge. It was this knowledge that made it possible for Job to wholeheartedly repent and receive God. It was when he repented that this restoration came.

Child of God, you can today recognize the work of Jesus on the cross. Our mediator made it possible for us to approach God. When we pray, we end the prayer with the prefix: In Jesus name Amen! The name of Jesus is the ticket that enables us to enter into a relationship with God. The blood of Jesus washes us clean from all unrighteousness. The death of Jesus on the cross takes away our sufferings and death to give us eternal life. The poverty of Jesus brings us into eternal prosperity. There is restoration for you. The daysman Jesus Christ made it possible.

CHAPTER 7

WEALTH AND POVERTY
- The Sharp Contrast

We have already said that Job was very wealthy. In the world of today and in the future, greatness is determined by wealth. We must appreciate the fact that wealth is a gift from God.

> *"Every man also to whom God had*
> *given riches and wealth, and hath given*
> *him power to eat thereof, and to take*
> *his portion, and to rejoice in his labour;*
> *this is the gift of God"*
> *Ecclesiastes 5:19*

Job was the richest man in the then known world. God gave him all these things, when the devil appeared on the scene, he lost everything. God restored him after nine months.

> *"Charge them that are rich in this world,*
> *that they be not highminded,*
> *nor trust in uncertain riches,*
> *but in the living God, who giveth*
> *us richly all things to enjoy ..."*
> *1 Timothy 6: 17-19*

The above quoted scripture has settled some issues and place some advice on record for the rich. Here are some commandments for the rich:

- ❖ ***Do not be arrogant.*** Many people allow pride to take hold of them. They look at wealth and riches and feel that it is by their power that they have obtained so much wealth. Many people forget so easily that it is God who gives us power to make wealth. They expect to be treated with higher respect because of their wealth.

- ❖ ***Do not put your hope or trust in riches.*** The wealth and riches of this world are uncertain. Job realized that wealth is uncertain. Our trust should be in the giver of the wealth and not in the wealth.

  > *"... riches certainly make themselves wings; they fly away as an eagle toward heaven".*
  > *Proverbs 23:5*

  > *"He that trusteth in his riches shall fall: but the righteous shall flourish as a branch"*
  > *Proverbs 11:28*

  > *"If riches increase, set not your heart upon them"*
  > *Psalm 62:10*

- ❖ ***Trust in the living God.*** The wealth giver deserves to be trusted. God declares that the silver and gold is his, He is to be trusted.

- ❖ ***Be rich in good deeds.*** God expects those he has prospered to use the wealth for good deeds. Good deeds include to contribute to the propagation of the gospel worldwide, to assist fellow Christians by meeting their needs. Giving to the poor, providing food and clothing to the destitute, widows and orphans are all classified as good deeds.

- ❖ ***Be ready to distribute and communicate in good things.*** This is to be liberal. Job was very liberal. The account in Job Chapter 29 ascertain this:

> *"There is that scattereth, and yet increaseth,*
> *and there is that withholdeth more than*
> *is meet, but it tendeth to poverty.*
> *The liberal soul shall be made fat:*
> *and he that watereth shall be watered*
> *also himself"*
> *Proverbs 11:24-25*

Release is the key to increase. Withholding leads to poverty. Do not stop giving when under financial stress. By keeping to these five commandments, the rich lay up treasures for themselves in heaven, and lay hold on eternal life (1 Timothy 6:19). Job knew that it is God that gives wealth. It is God that gives the increase.

> *"But thou shalt remember the Lord thy God:*
> *for it is he that giveth thee power to get wealth ..."*
> *Deuteronomy 8:18*

The Problems of Wealth

Wealth is good. God gives wealth. If we should recognize God as the giver of wealth and reverence him, there will be no problem. The first problem associated with wealth is that men become greedy too easily. When they become greedy, they tend to worship the wealth rather than the giver of wealth.

> *"No man can serve two masters:*
> *for either he will hate the one and*
> *love the other; or else he will hold to*
> *the one and despise the other. Ye*
> *cannot serve God and mammon"*
> *Matthew 6:24*

Mammon in the above scripture refers to riches. Serving anything outside of God the Creator is idolatry, and is as bad as serving Satan.

Some people want wealth so much that they could do anything to get wealth. We have heard of husbands sacrificing their wives to get wealth.

> *"... And they say, How doth God know?*
> *and is there knowledge in the Most High?*
> *Behold, these are the ungodly, who prosper*
> *in the world: they increase in riches".*
> *Psalm 73: 4-13*

> *"They are waxen fat, they shine;*
> *Yea, they overpass the deeds of the wicked ...*
> *Shall I not visit for these things? ...*
> *A wonderful and horrible*
> *thing is committed in the land"*
> *Jeremiah 5: 28-30*

> *"But godliness with contentment*
> *is great gain. For we brought*
> *nothing into this world ...*
>
> *For the love of money is the*
> *root of all evil which while some*
> *coveted after, they have*
> *erred from the faith, and pierced*
> *Themselves through with many sorrows".*
> *1 Timothy 6: 6-10*

In the above popular scripture, we understand that:

- All men do not love money only some do.
- Money is not evil, only the love of money is. The unhealthy desire for money is evil.
- The spirit of covetousness can creep into the mind of man when he starts to love money.
- Money could be a means of blessing or a curse depending on how it is handled.

Solomon wrote in Ecclesiastes 5:13

"There is a sore evil which I have seen under the sun, namely, riches kept for the owners thereof to their hurt".

❖ **Money is important.** Your money represents you. It represents your time, skills, zeal, talents, abilities and your work. Your money represents your life's blood. How you spend your money is important to God. If you freely give your money to God, then y o u   a r e giving yourself.

❖ People who think that they must have an expensive home, drive an expensive car, wear expensive clothes, constantly long and strive to acquire more money and riches in this world are controlled by the spirit of covetousness. Their money and worldly possessions have become their priority.

In the parable of the rich fool, Jesus told the story of the rich young man that was held captive by the spirit of covetousness. The perspective that God wants you to have concerning your money is the kingdom perspective. The world perspective of money is:

- Get as much money as you can.
- Spend as much money as you can for yourself
- Store up as much money as you can in the banks/investments

In the contrary, the kingdom perspective of money is:

- God is the source of all your monies/and finances.
- Give your money freely and liberally to God and men as God directs.
- Store up treasures in heaven not earthly riches.
- Be contented at all times.

Greed is sin. It can lead to more sin. It is the sin of the rich and the poor.

> *"A faithful man shall*
> *abound with blessings:*
> *but he that maketh haste to*
> *be rich shall not be innocent"*
> *Proverbs 28:20*

> *"Your riches are corrupted and your*
> *garments are motheaten. Behold,*
> *the hire of the laborers who have*
> *reaped down your fields, which is of you*
> *kept back by fraud, crieth ...*
> *Ye have condemned and killed the just;*
> *And he doth not resist you".*
> *James 5:2-6*

All evil rich men shall face the wrath of God. Their riches shall be corrupted. Their silver and gold cankered. The rust of poison of their riches shall witness against them before God. Their riches shall be transferred to the just. This is the restoration of the church.

> *"As the patridge sitteth on eggs, and hatcheth them not; so he that getteth riches, and not by right, shall leave them in the midst of his days, and at his end shall be a fool".*
> *Jeremiah 17:11*

> *"A good man leaveth an inheritance to his children's children: and the wealth of the sinner is laid up for the just."*
> *Proverbs 13:22*

We shall revisit the issue of wealth transfer in the chapter on restoration.

The Problem of Poverty:

Poverty is the desperate shortage of spending power. Poverty cannot easily be eradicated. Poverty is a destroyer.

> *"The rich man's wealth is his strong city: The destruction of the poor is their poverty"*
> *Proverbs 10:15*

> *"For the poor shall never cease out of the land..."*
> *Deuteronomy 15:11*

> *"For ye have the poor always with you,..."*
> *Matthew 26:11*

There would always be poor people everywhere. Poverty leads to the destruction of the poor. Take a look at Africa, malaria kills millions of African children annually. Life expectancy has been reduced to 40 whereas the same for Europe is 75. The destruction of the poor is their poverty. A child that eats palm kernel, stones and water for dinner cannot be bright in the school compared to the one that eats one egg everyday. This is one of the problems of poverty.

Poor people subconsciously get used to poverty and want to remain there. Even after being born again, poor people still remain poor. It takes a lot knowledge, will, faith and action to come out of poverty.

By the sin of Adam, we were all born into poverty. Prosperity started with the Abrahamic covenant but was perfected by the blood of Jesus. Many Christians are still living in ignorance abject poverty and frustration. Many people are poor because they have accepted to be poor.

Examples of poverty abound in the Bible: Gideon (Judges 6:6); The widow of Zerephath (1 Kings 17:12); A certain widow (2 Kings 4:1) etc. Poverty could be self-inflicted or inherited. Whatever the cause of poverty may be, there is a way out for the believer.

Job, our main character in this book experienced poverty, sickness, disease, etc. but he re-discovered himself and overcame poverty. You too can overcome poverty.
(Further readings: Proverbs 28:19; Isaiah 3:14; Acts 11:28; Luke 10:30)

GOD is Generous

We can see that God is a giver, generous and benevolent. Job was a generous man. Poverty is far from prosperity. One is the opposite of the other. If we were made in the image of the Almighty God, then we must be like him.
God expects us to be generous this is the bridge that takes one from poverty to prosperity. Generosity is the pivot for which durable riches could be sustained.

> *"Give to him that asketh thee and from him*
> *that would borrow of thee turn not thou away"*
> *Matthew 5:42*

> *"As we have therefore opportunity,*
> *let us do good unto all men, especially unto*
> *them who are of the household of faith"*
> *Galatians 6:10*

Can you be generous if you are poor? Yes! There is nobody that has nothing to give out. Why not ask God to bless you so that you can be generous.

CHAPTER 8

THE RESTORATION OF MAN

The book of Job could easily pass for the documentations of wisdom. Job knew that his change would come.

*"If a man die, shall he live again?
all the days of my appointed time
will I wait, till my change come".
Job 14:14*

*"For there is hope for a tree,
if it be cut down that it will sprout again,
and that the tender branch thereof will not cease".
Job 14:7*

*"For I know that my redeemer
liveth, and that he shall stand at the latter
day upon the earth.
And though after my skin worms
destroy this body, yet in my flesh shall I see God ..."
Job 19: 25-27*

*"When men are cast down, then thou shalt
say, there is lifting up; ..."
Job 22:29*

Despite all the odds that Job went through, he knew that his restoration would come. By the restoration of Job, God established that:

⇨ It is possible to restore man irrespective of his affliction.

⇨ Restoration takes a very short time, past affliction is easily forgotten because of the joy of restoration.

⇨ Job believed that there will be a restoration and he kept reiterating that conviction until it came to reality.

God promises us restoration. Restoration means to put back in office or give back what was originally yours. The complete work of Jesus was to restore man. From the fall of Adam to the cross of Jesus, man lost his rightful place; but Jesus has restored man. The word of God gave a promise for restoration.

*"And I will restore to you the
years that the locust hath eaten,
the cankerworm, and the caterpillar,
and the palmerworm...
and ye shall eat in plenty and be satisfied..."
Joel 2: 25-26*

*"They shall be carried to Babylon,
and there shall they be until the
day that I visit them ... then will I bring
them up, and restore them to this place"
Jeremiah 27:22*

*"For I will restore health unto thee,
and I will heal thee of thy wounds,
said the Lord; ..." Jeremiah 30:17*

Restoration is normally carried out in folds: single, double, seven folds, etc. Which one would you settle for? If you are down today, you can call your restoration to be. **It is possible. Jesus made it possible for you!**

Pre-requisite for Restoration

To establish the prerequisite for restoration, a look at our main character in this book Job. The following points are worthy of note:

✡   **Repentance**

> *"... Wherefore I abhor myself,*
> *and repent in dust and ashes".*
> *Job 42:3-6*

Job repented of all his utterances and asked God for forgiveness. There must be repentance before restoration. Please note that Job was not to repent from adultery, drunkenness or murder, but repented of uttering he did not understand.

> *"... except ye repent,*
> *ye shall all likewise perish"*
> *Luke 13:3*

Repentance brings you into relationship with God.

> *"Behold the Lord's hand is not shortened,*
> *that it cannot save; neither his ear heavy*
> *that it cannot hear: but your iniquities have*

> *separated between you and your God,*
> *and your sins have hid his face*
> *from you, that he will not hear: ...*
> *your lips have spoken lies, your tongue*
> *hath muttered perverseness".*
> *Isaiah 59:1-3*

✡ **Job forgave his friends**. God was not happy with Job's friends. They were to repent before Job. God commanded that they present an offering/sacrifice before Job.

> *"And the Lord turned the captivity*
> *of Job, when he prayed for his friends ..."*
> *Job 42:10*

> *"And forgive us our debts, as*
> *we forgive our debtors.... For if ye*
> *forgive men their trespasses,*
> *your heavenly Father will also*
> *forgive you". Matthew 6:12-15*

Job also forgave his friends when his friends repented before him. It is important to forgive others especially when we require God's blessing.

✡ **Job asked for God's mercy**. The mercy seat of God is never vacant.

The latter End of Job:

The truth is that God restored Job.

> *"So the Lord blessed the latter*
> *end of Job more than his beginning ..."*
> *Job 42:12a*

Job enjoyed a two-fold restoration. If we look at the restoration of Job, we could be able to highlight the following points:

☐   Job enjoyed favour from his brothers and sister.

> *"For thou, Lord, wilt bless the*
> *righteous: with favour wilt*
> *thou compass him as with a shield"*
> *Psalm 5:12*

> *"Then came there unto him all*
> *his brethren, and all his sisters, and*
> *all they that had been of his acquaintance*
> *before, and did eat bread with him ...*
> *and comforted him over all the evil ...*
> *every man also gave him a piece of money,*
> *and everyone an earring of gold".*
> *Job 42:11*

The same brothers and sisters that abandoned Job during his nine months of captivity came back to him with gifts. They brought money and gold to Job. All the things Job had after his captivity was given to him. The same men were around but could not help him because it was not yet time for his restoration.

- The end of Job was a two-fold restoration. All the material possessions he had before the trials were doubled.

> *"... for he had fourteen thousand sheep, and six thousand sheep, and six thousand camels, and a thousand yoke of oxen, and a thousand she asses".*
> *Job 42:12b*

- The number of his children restored.

> *"He had also seven sons and three daughters".*
> *Job 42:13*

In due season, God restored Job with the number of his children.

- Job's daughters were very beautiful.

> *"And in all the land were no women found so fair as the daughters of Job:..."*
> *Job 42:15*

Job's three daughters called Jemima, Kezia and Keren happuch. Jemima resembling a clear day, fair as the day literal for a dove. Kezia or Cassia after one of the most valuable and fragrant spices of antiquity. Keren-happuch, born of the eye-paint. This refers to a vessel made of horn where the oriental women keep their eye pencil and paints. The make-up makes the women to appear more beautiful and attractive.

☐ Job lived a long life. This is the real restoration.

> *"After this lived Job an hundred*
> *and forty years, and saw his sons,*
> *and his sons' sons, even four generations"*
> *Job 42:16*

Job did not only raise his children, but also his grand children. He fulfilled the scripture in Proverbs 13:22:

> *"A good man liveth an inheritance*
> *to his children's children..."*

☐ Job enjoyed fellowship with God after his trials. God called him his servant (Job 42:8). If you are a servant of God, then you can be restored. Restoration is your portion. Many people have lost many things in this life. What do you want restored? What have you lost money, time, opportunities, houses, etc. This is the time for restoration. How many fold restoration do you want. God wants to restore you today! Talk to God for your restoration now.

CHAPTER 9

THE GREAT QUESTIONS

Where is God? Sometimes our perception of God can make us miss God's presence. Especially when somebody is under pressure and expects God to appear on the scene, and perhaps the contrary happens he will ask the question where is God? Many believers have asked themselves can God deliver the righteous? I have seen some people ask the question why me?

When you step into some circumstances and you see the incidences that Satan has caused to happen to you, you cannot help, but ask the question Why me? Why? Where is God? What sin have I committed to deserve this severe suffering? Some situations are really pitiable poverty, homelessness, suffering, starvation, penury, disappointment, nakedness, hunger, untimely death. Some of these conditions could be very pathetic. Many people Christians have had cause to cry for days due to some pathetic occurrences. You ask me Is God listening? Why does he allow us to be tempted? Is God fair in the distribution of troubles?

> *"Dominion and fear are with him,*
> *he maketh peace in high places ...*
>
> *How then can man be justified*
> *with God? or how can he be*
> *clean that is born of a woman? ...*
> *How much less man, that is a worm?*

and the son of man which is a worm?"
Job 25:2-6

"Although thou sayest thou shalt not see him, yet judgement is before him: therefore trust thou in him".
Job 35:14

"All nations before him are as nothing; and they are counted to him less than nothing, and vanity"
Isaiah 40:17

"For the eyes of the Lord run to and fro throughout the whole earth, to shew himself strong in the behalf of them whose heart is perfect toward him..."
2Chronicles 16:9a

As a child, I asked God a few questions. When our earthly father died on 28th December 1975, I was only thirteen

God is always there. He does not change location or go on transfer. He is the creator of the earth. Nothing takes him by surprise. He sees the people suffering. He hears their cries. Why does he not move with compassion towards the suffering Christian? Why does God allow armed robbers to kill a Christian? God is holy. Why does he allow girls to commit abortion? Harlots are all over on the streets of major cities of the world Lagos, Milan Ontario, etc. Car snatching is a common occurrence in today's world. Is God having a good time watching these nasty occurrences?

years old. Seven children left behind I was number three in the hierarchy. My uncle (contrary to the native tradition) seized all my father's belongings and threw my mother (with seven children) out of the family home. We wept sore! My mother cried for 12 months before realizing what had happened. She asked God questions- "Why should I be the one to live? Why did all of us not die at the same time? What should I do with seven children? God kill me or won't you?" Onlookers wept sore!

My school band (St. Vincent's Secondary School band) made an appearance at the burial ceremony this was the only colourful part of the pain. The teachers and all the students joined my mother in questioning God. Our questions would make up at least twenty volumes. The villagers joined in the questioning. I thought (as a child) that God would appear to defend himself. He did not. The position of things today makes us know that God is our restoration.

Some Facts about GOD:

Christianity has developed over the years. Many years ago, nobody dares to find out details about God. This book will commit a few things to paper about God to enable us understand the plan of God for humanity.

The following facts about God will help us to understand the book of Job better:

- God is a person (Job 13:8; Hebrews 1:3)
- God has a spirit body (Daniel 7: 9-14; Isaiah 6; Ezekiel 1)

- God has an image and likeness (Genesis 1:26; 9:6; James 3:9)
- God has hands, fingers and heart. (Genesis 6:6; Psalm 102:25-26; Revelation 5: 1-7)
- God has a mouth, a tongue and lips (Isaiah 11:4; Numbers 12:8)
- God has a head, hair, arms and feet (Exodus 24:10; Daniel 7:9; Ezekiel 1:26-28)
- God has a countenance. (Psalm 11:7)
- God could express anger, jealousy, hate, pity, love, fellowship and any of the emotions. (Proverbs 6:16; 1 Kings 11:9; Exodus 20:5; John 3:16; Psalm 103:13; 1 John 1:1-7)
- God has a will. (Romans 8:27; 9:19)
- God is knowledge and wisdom. (Isaiah 11:2)
- He sits on the throne (Isaiah 6; Daniel 7: 9-11)

Some Attributes of God

"Thy mercy, O Lord is in the heavens; and thy faithfulness reacheth unto the clouds"
Psalm 36:5

We need to highlight some of the attributes of God to enable us discuss the book of Job and the role of God in time of suffering. The following could be deduced from Psalm 36:

➢ Mercy high as the heavens (verse 5)
➢ Faithfulness far reaching as the clouds (verse 5)
➢ Righteousness high as mountains (verse 8)

- ➤ Justice deep as the abyss (verse 6)
- ➤ Preservation universal as existence (verse 6)
- ➤ Excellent kindness (verse 7)
- ➤ Providence the complete requirement (verse 8)
- ➤ Satisfaction rivers of pleasure (verse 9)
- ➤ Life God is the fountain of life (verse 9)
- ➤ Light the source of the truth (verse 9)

The ten attributes of God shall be used in understanding his operations and dealings with man. We need to understand a few things about God so that we would not be in the same shoes with Job.

Pain and Suffering:

The word "suffering" is otherwise called affliction or pain. The root word in Hebrew language is **ra**. This means bad, evil, adversity, affliction, calamity, grief and sorrow. The word is also used in most Bible translations for wretchedness. It is never used for sin. Even though Bible scholars all over the world believe that God made sorrow, misery, weeping, pain, etc. as the sure fruit of sin, He made the law of sowing and reaping. This law is constant upon the earth 'as long as the earth remaineth'.

In the case of Job, it was used for physical and spiritual calamities. Most of the time the word "afflict" refers to spiritual suffering. Out of 177 times that the word 'afflict' appear in the King James Version of the Holy Bible, only six times does it refer to physical suffering or pain:

THE GREAT QUESTIONS   The Revelation of Restoration

> *"Many are the afflictions of the righteous*
> *but the Lord delivereth him out of them all"*
> *Psalm 34:19*

General Facts about Suffering: It would be good to know the following about suffering:

⇨ God regulates affliction, suffering or pain according to the law of sowing and reaping (Psalm 80:5, Isaiah 9:1)

⇨ God determines the length of every affliction. In the case of Job, it was nine months. The length of the affliction also depends on the reaction of the person suffering it to the circumstances. (Genesis 15: 13-14; Numbers 14:33)

⇨ Sometimes, afflictions are not sent willingly to men. It depends on the circumstances - the plans of God for the man and the accusations leveled against him by the devil. (Lamentations 3:33)

⇨ Due to the sin of Adam, men are born into affliction. When Adam sinned against God, poverty set in, then sickness, then and death. All men in the first Adam are born to suffer.

> *"Although affliction cometh not forth*
> *of the dust, neither doth trouble spring*
> *out of the ground; yet man is born unto*

> *trouble, as the sparks fly upward".*
> *Job 5:6-7*

⇨ Saints have been appointed to see afflictions. The truth is that saints shall see many afflictions. These will not kill them but God will make a way for them.

> *"... In the world ye*
> *shall have tribulation:*
> *but be of good cheer, I have*
> *overcome the world".*
> *John 16:33*

⇨ Severe afflictions are as a result of curses not doing the right thing.

⇨ Friends, associates, self and on-lookers often misinterpret afflictions - The case of Job is an example.

⇨ Many Christians are purged during trials, temptations and afflictions.

⇨ Afflictions are temporary. They shall always pass away. All we need to do is persevere.

Based on the teachings of the Bible, the following conditions cause afflictions to come upon a man:

- Sin of all sizes and shapes (Gen. 3:16; Psalm 25: 18)
- Backsliding (Psalm 119:67)
- Misuse of the tongue (already discussed) Proverbs 26:28

- Resentment (Genesis 16: 4-16)
- Pride/arrogance (Job 33: 14-29)
- Impenitence (Proverbs 1: 30-31; Rev. 2:21)
- Born into affliction/curses (Job 5:6)
- Maltreatment of others (Genesis 27: 1-46; 32:11)
- Hardness of heart (Exodus 4-12)
- Idolatry (Judges 10:6-10: 2 Kings 17)
- Forgetting God (1 Samuel 12: 9-10)
- Hypocrisy (Matthew 23)

In the case of Job, he was basically ignorant of the existence of Satan and this led to some of the sins he committed. Be this as it may, Job used his tongue roughly, he was ignorant of God's plan and manifested to be a hypocrite. Job was ignorant of the devices of the enemy. God must have reason(s) for allowing man to see tribulation and affliction.

Reasons for Affliction:

God is a God of purpose. God allows afflictions to befall man for the following reasons:

(a) To work good in man and bring him to perfection. (Psalm 119:71)

(b) To hide or extinguish pride from man. (Job 33:14-29)

(c) To demonstrate God's faithfulness; as he always solve the problem (Psalm 119:75)

(d) To test the sincerity of man. (Job 1-2; James 5: 10-11)

(e) To refine, purify and increase man's faithfulness to God (Isaiah 48:10; John 15:2; Hebrews 12: 10-11)

(f) To increase the spiritual power of man after passing through the test. (Romans 5:1-8; James 1:2-4; 4:7)

(g) To humble man and bring him back to God. (Psalm 89: 30-32; Hebrews 12:5)

(h) To make man learn obedience and truth (Psalm 119:71; Hebrews 5:8)

(I) To manifest love and affection. (Proverbs 3: 11-12; Hebrews 12: 5-10)

(j) To give reward (Romans 8:17; 2 Cor. 4:17)

Most times, afflictions are stepping stones for upliftment.

Affliction could manifest in various forms. This include hunger, starvation, penury, nakedness, frustration, poverty, sickness, disease, family troubles, barrenness, imprisonment, physical sufferings, etc. A man in trouble needs help; can one find God when in trouble?

The Promise of GOD

What is the promise of God during affliction?
Contrary to popular opinion, God does not just watch the believer suffer. He is interested in seeing the believer out of every temptation. The following are some of the promises of God regarding those under affliction:

THE GREAT QUESTIONS   The Revelation of Restoration

- God will hear the afflicted. That is why what we say when under affliction matters. It is better to speak healing and deliverance when under affliction.

> *"So that they cause the cry of the poor*
> *to come unto him, and he heareth*
> *the cry of the afflicted"*
> *Job 34:28*

- God will save the afflicted (Psalm 18:27)

- God will have mercy on the afflicted.

> *"Sing, O heavens; and be joyful,*
> *O earth; and break forth into singing,*
> *O mountains; for the Lord hath comforted*
> *his people and will have mercy upon his afflicted".*
> *Isaiah 49:13*

- God will deliver the afflicted from fear (Psalm 23:4)

- God will deliver the afflicted from all their troubles.
  - ✺ God desires that we defeat the devil on a daily basis.

> *"And call upon me in the day of*
> *trouble I will deliver thee and*
> *thou shalt glorify me"*
> *Psalm 50:15*

- God will uphold the afflicted.

THE GREAT QUESTIONS   The Revelation of Restoration

> *"Cast thy burden upon the Lord, and he shall sustain thee: he shall never suffer the righteous to be moved".*
> *Psalm 55:22*

☐ God will reward the afflicted.

> *"Blessed are they which are persecuted for righteousness' sake: for theirs is the kingdom of heaven".*
> *Matthew 5:10*

☐ God has promised to be a refuge to the afflicted.

> *"The Lord will also be a refuge for the oppressed, a refuge in times of trouble"*
> *Psalm 9:9*

☐ The Lord will remember the weakness of the afflicted. He will hide them and consider the afflicted.

> *"I will be glad and rejoice in thy mercy: for thou hast considered my trouble: thou hast known my soul in adversities; ..."*
> *Psalm 31:7*

☐ During afflictions, God will make his manifold grace available to you.

> *"... My grace is sufficient for thee:*
> *for my strength is made perfect in*
> *weakness. Most gladly therefore will*
> *I rather glory in my infirmities,*
> *that the power of Christ may rest upon me..."*
> *2 Corinthians 12:9-10*

Suffering and pain is a difficult area to talk to someone about. Any man under pain or affliction requires help. The truth has been established that God is good and cannot do wrong.

> *"Yea, surely God will not do wickedly,*
> *neither with the Almighty pervert*
> *Judgement"*
> *Job 34: 12*

The book of Job has also established that God can speak to man. The purpose of God speaking to man is to guide man in the right track. For believers all over the world, we know that trials, temptations, afflictions help us to get our promotions, if only we know this, then our reactions, and utterances during afflictions would be guided.

> *"To bring back his soul from*
> *the pit, to be enlightened with*
> *the light of the living".*
> *Job 33:30*

God being who he is just and holy - will punish and reward fairly in this life and hereafter.

> *"... Lord God Almighty, true and righteous*
> *are thy judgements"*
> *Revelations 16:7*

In all cases, God requires the faith of man to decide the duration of his suffering and trials. You can rise to the occasion. Are you under any form of suffering, hardship or pain? The truth is revealed here for you. Make up your mind and walk out of the test now! God has not left you alone.

CHAPTER 10

HYPOCRISY - THE GREATEST SIN

*I*n the book of Job, we find out that all Job's friends called Job a hypocrite. This must be serious. Could this be the reason why Job's restoration was not immediate? Was Job complacent?

"How can man be justified with God?
or how can he be clean that is born of a woman?"
Job 25:4

"For the congregation of hypocrites shall be desolate
and fire shall consume the tabernacles of bribery"
Job 15:34

"But the hypocrite in heart heap up wrath:
they cry not when he bindeth them".
Job 36:13

"For what is the hope of the hypocrite, though he
hath gained, when God taketh away his soul?"
Job 27:8

Elihu, the daysman also rebuked Job of self righteousness.

"For Job hath said, I am righteous: and
God hath taken away my judgement,..."
Job 34: 5-9

God also called Job, a hypocrite.

> *"Wilt thou also disannul my judgement? Wilt thou condemn me, that thou mayest be righteous?"*
> *Job 40:8*

The word of God cannot be broken. Out of the mouth of two or three witnesses will the word be established. Eliphaz, Bildad, Zophar, Elihu and God called Job a hypocrite in this story. Please note that before his affliction, Job was seen as "perfect" before God. Hypocrisy entered into Job during the period of his affliction.

However, the point has been made. A man born into Adam can never be just in the sight of God, for Job to attempt to justify himself before the Almighty was equivalent to striving with God. The reason is that there was no perfect sacrifice at this time for the remission of sins. As a sinner, you are judged in the death of Jesus on the cross. The death of Jesus sets aside the reckoned condemnation for ever. Any attempt by a mortal man to justify himself in God's presence without the covering of the blood of Jesus amounts to self-righteousness and therefore hypocrisy.

Job tried to justify himself in Adam (Read Job Chapter 29). On many occasions, Job challenged God to show him his errors. (We have already treated this in Chapter Five of this book). He accused God of being responsible for his suffering. Job was really under pressure. We can call him an ignorant hypocrite. God views hypocrisy seriously. Here were some of Job's utterances when under affliction:

> *"Thou knowest that I am not wicked: and there is none that can deliver out of thine hand. Thine hands have made me and fashioned me together round about; yet thou dost destroy me".*
> *Job 10:7-8*

> *"Wherefore hidest thou thy face, and holdest me for thine enemy?"*
> *Job 13:24*

> *"I am clean without transgression, I am innocent; neither is there iniquity in me".*
> *Job 33:9*

Hypocrites - who are they?

Job acknowledged the fact that he could be justified before God (hypocrisy).

> *"I know it is so of a truth: but how should a man be just with God? If he will contend with him ... He is wise in heart and mighty in strength, who hath hardened himself against him and hath prospered?"*
> *Job 9:1-3*

HYPOCRISY - THE GREATEST SIN

Job reasoned that if someone contended with God, it would be difficult for a man to answer the charges of God. He opined that God could charge a man with a thousand sins. The meaning is that man could not answer the charges of God. Man's sins are many and could be counted in thousands.

Hypocrisy is defined by Jesus in Matthew 6:2:

> *"Therefore when thou doest thine alms, do not sound a trumpet before thee, as the hypocrites do in the synagogues and in the streets, that they may have glory of men ..."*

Basically, hypocrites are actors under a mask. Hypocrites operate by feigning principles and feel no passion for their actions. They literally sound trumpets under the pretext of calling the poor with the design of self-gratification by giving alms in public. The hypocrites profess to love what they do not love, try to find pleasure in what their hearts hate. They mingle with people with whom they have no sympathy for. They partake in religious activities when their hearts are not there.

Wow! There are multitudes of hypocrites in the Christendom today. Old Christians without testimonies are hypocrites. Religious men and women who tell tales of early Christianity, and do not enjoy daily refreshing in the word of God are hypocrites. Some people go to church so that the pastor can see them not because of the message. In big churches, Elders and deacons have constituted themselves to be the hypocrites, many married women go to church to check out the latest fashion designs, gossip about young girls' dressings and tell tales of husbands' habits. This is hypocrisy.

Characteristics of Hypocrites:

Matthew Chapter 23 is one chapter of the Bible that deals with the subject of hypocrisy. If we follow this chapter closely, we will discover the following characteristics of hypocrites:

- They demand respect as teachers (verse 2).
- They teach, but do not practice what they teach. (verse 3)
- This is to say that hypocrites lack integrity because their word and action do not match.
- They always demand service from men. They do not equally give the service (verse 4).
- They always seek the praise of men and not that of God. (verse 5)
- They use religion as means of personal gains (Mark 7:11-12)
- Their religion is physical and lack spiritual depth (verse 5)
- They lack humility, they occupy the chief places at feast and in the church (verse 6).
- They display their tithes (verse 7).

HYPOCRISY - THE GREATEST SIN

- They hold onto the traditions of men in preference to God's word. (Mark 7: 12-13)
- They glory in personal attention; seek personal recognition. They will not wait for events to take their turn (verse 6).
- They rob men of truth and life (verse 13).
- They take undue advantage of widows, orphans and the poor in the society (verse 14).
- They exhibit prototype forms of prayers with long quoted scriptures (already prepared in their minds) verse 14.
- They are zealous to win men to their sect. Many hypocrites do not attend evening teachings in the church but would not miss community meeting or men's fellowship meeting. They are eager to win men to their sect than win them to Christ. (verse 15)
- Profess to be the light yet dwells in darkness. They are blind to truth and practical Christianity (verse 16-22)
- Propagates the incomplete Gospel especially the part that brings honour to them.
- Stress minor details and omits the higher details. They honour God with their lips and not with their hearts.
- Exhibit outward religion (dressing, covering of hair, fasting, etc.) and omit the fundamentals repentance, forgiveness, holiness, meditation (verse 23-25).
- Pretend to be more righteous than their forefathers (verses 29-33)

HYPOCRISY - THE GREATEST SIN

There are many hypocrites in our churches today. Many times, they remain in the church and new comers get miracles the hypocrites get nothing. God hates hypocrisy. In the earthly ministry of Jesus, he did not hide his feelings about them. God hates dependence upon an outward show of religion and claiming protection/deliverance from God because of such rites.

> *"Cry aloud, and spare not, lift up thy voice like a trumpet, and shew my people their transgression and the house of Jacob their sins. Yet they seek me daily, and delight to know my ways as a nation that did righteousness, and forsook not the ordinance of their God ...*
>
> *Wherefore have we fasted, say they, and thou seest not?*
> *Wherefore have we afflicted our soul and thou takest no knowledge?*
> *Behold, in the day of your fast ye find pleasure, and exact all your labours.*
> *Behold, ye fast for strife and debate, and to smite with the fist of wickedness: ye shall not fast as ye Do this day to make your voice to be heard on high".*
> *Isaiah 58:1-4*

Hypocrites seek God daily as a routine and an outward show of attraction to self and deceive others. They pretend to delight to know God's ways. They are religious men and women they carry out a lot of rituals. They are always careful about the physical display rather than the spiritual attachments. They think that outward religion pleases God. I have heard some people pray and ask God could you remind me of a day I did not come to church? **The number of times you go to church does not matter like the number of revelations you have received into your spirit.**

Hypocrites (as shown in Isaiah 58) complain that God ignores their fasts, and strict compliance to the observation of the rituals. They challenge God for complacency in their troubles. To the new converts, they paint themselves as those that could predict God's action due to long period of interaction with him. God is not pleased with the fast of the hypocrite. Strife, contention and display of fasting obligation is not acceptable in God's sight.

When you lack integrity, you are a hypocrite. When your words and your actions do not match, you are a hypocrite. Jesus said that hypocrisy is the greatest sin; Job was not one before his trials. During the period of trials, alongside with his friends, he thought that he should have known God better, he fell into hypocrisy. Hypocrites cannot obtain miracles from God. Job's restoration only came after his repentance.

The Dangers of Hypocrisy

Hypocrisy is dangerous as we can see in this chapter. We cannot also say that these people are rare, they are all around us. Even some of you reading this book are hypocrites. You can change! If your life has lacked daily miracles or if your Christianity has been a matter of routine you may be the one to change. Hypocrisy is dangerous for any Christian. At the time Jesus walked the earth he branded the Pharisees, scribes and Sadducees hypocrites. These were the teachers of the law. The scribes were the ones to recopy the scrolls that later became the Bible. This is the greatest sin. Many people are involved here. The degree of hypocrisy varies from person to person. Check through the twenty characteristics of hypocrites and make peace with God today. This is the sin of the believer.

We shall give you a few points here to show you that hypocrisy is dangerous for you as a child of God.

➢ God will not have mercy on hypocrites Even though he is a merciful God. Can any man survive this life without God's mercy?

> *"Therefore the Lord shall have no*
> *joy in their young men, neither shall*
> *have mercy on their fatherless and widows:*
> *For everyone is an hypocrite and an*
> *evil doer, and every mouth speaketh folly ..."*
> *Isaiah 9:17*

➢ There is no hope for the hypocrite. To the hypocrite, life is hopeless.

HYPOCRISY - THE GREATEST SIN

> *"For what is the hope of the hypocrite,*
> *though he hath gained, when God*
> *taketh away his soul?"*
> *Job 27:8*

What is life without hope?

- The hypocrites will not obtain any reward for serving God.

  > *"For the vile person will speak villany,*
  > *and his heart will work iniquity,*
  > *to practise hypocrisy, and to utter*
  > *error against the Lord to make empty*
  > *the soul of the hungry and he will*
  > *cause the drink of the thirsty to fail"*
  > *Isaiah 32:6*

- Hypocrites are the accusers of men.

  > *"Thou hypocrite, first cast out the beam*
  > *out of thine own eye; and then shalt*
  > *thou see clearly to cast out*
  > *the mote out of thy brother's eye"*
  > *Matthew 7:5*

- Hypocrites always justify themselves. They render mainly lip service to men.

HYPOCRISY - THE GREATEST SIN

*"For thou hast said: My doctrine is pure,
and I am clean in thy eyes" Job 11:4
"Even so ye also outwardly appear
righteous unto men,
but within ye are full of hypocrisy
and iniquity". Matthew 23:28*

The Bible warns us to flee from hypocrisy. Unfortunately, many hypocrites do not know that they are one. There is need for self-assessment all the time to ascertain our position in this matter.

➢ All hypocrites are under a curse. They will suffer with the wicked. Matthew Chapter 23 defined hypocrites as almost being synonymous with scribes and Pharisees. This chapter of the Bible has five times said "woe" to the hypocrites which means that the hypocrites are under a curse.

*"Woe unto you ... hypocrites for ye are
as graves which appear not". Luke 11:44*

➢ God knows the hypocrites. He knows all things. We should be careful how we try to deceive God.

*"... But he knowing their hypocrisy
said unto them why tempt ye me?".
Mark 12:15*

From the above analysis, we see that man is guilty, mortal man has no righteousness in him. Any man standing before

God as his judge is guilty. God has found a ransom in Jesus. In Jesus, we are justified; the blood of Jesus makes us a new creation. With Jesus, we have righteousness in God; without him, we are hopelessly guilty. The righteousness of Jesus freely justifies us. The blood of Jesus can wash away any type or class of hypocrisy. When Job repented, he was restored. You can repent from all types of hypocrisy and let God give you a new spiritual experience. It is possible for you to be having daily miracles but God has to make it possible. He can make it possible for you to repent from acts of hypocrisy.

> *"Acquaint now thyself with him and be at peace: thereby good shall come unto thee"*
> *Job 22:21*

Conclusion

The book of Job is very interesting. There is one underlining factor that should be highlighted. Job was a descendant of Abraham therefore he was in Adam. All believers today are in Christ. This provides the major paradox of this drama, the old and the new which is better?

We read from the scriptures that God created man for himself. We look at ourselves and we desire to know why God created us. It could be distressing if we leave this earth without fulfilling the purpose why God called us. I am determined to fulfill the plan of God for my life. I want to believe that you would also want the purpose of God for your life to be fulfilled. Knowledge has increased. The increase in the knowledge of events and things is the result of what God is doing with us. You may have seen, heard and perceive multitude of things that make us realize that knowledge is on the increase. The end time is upon us!

> *"For the earth shall be filled with the knowledge of the glory of the Lord, as the waters cover the sea".*
> *Habakuk 2:14*

It is the increase in knowledge that has made this book a reality. I believe that after reading this book, you will be able to freely open to the book of Job and read it as any other book of the Bible. You are free from the fear of the book of Job in Jesus Name! Amen!

Conclusion   **The Revelation of Restoration**

As Adam is of the old covenant and Jesus Christ is of the new covenant, we shall look at some outstanding disparity between the old and the new to enable us conclude this book properly.

✵ In Adam we are all sinners; whereas in Christ we are made righteous.

> *"For all have sinned and come short of the glory of God…". Romans 3:23*
> *"For he hath made him to be sin for us, who knew no sin; that we might be made the righteousness of God in him"*
> *2 Corinthians 5:21*

You can avail yourself the opportunity and stand righteous before God in Christ.

✵ In Adam, we were doomed to sin, sickness and death. In Christ, we possess eternal life.

> *"Wherefore as by one man sin entered the world, and death by sin: and so death passed upon all men, for that all have sinned"*
> *Romans 5:12*

✵ In Adam, we were separated from God, whereas in Christ, we are reconciled to God.

Conclusion   The Revelation of Restoration

> *"That at that time we were without Chirst,
> being aliens from the commonwealth of
> Israel, and strangers from the covenants
> of promise having no hope and without
> God in the world But now in Christ Jesus,
> ye who sometimes were far off are
> made nigh by the blood of Christ"*
> *Ephesians 2:12-13*

✲ In Adam, we partook of our fallen nature whereas in Christ we partake of his divine nature.

> *"Wherein in time past ye walked according
> to the course of this world, according to the
> prince of the power of the air, the
> spirit that now worketh in the
> children of disobedience..."*
> *Ephesians 2:2*

✲ In Adam, we are bound to constant turmoil, we had no rest. In Christ, we are free to enjoy eternal rest. It could not have been better!

> *"But the wicked are like the trouble sea,
> when it cannot rest whose waters cast up mire and dirt
> There is no peace, saith my God, to the wicked"*
> *Isaiah 57:20-21*

"For we which have believed do enter into rest,
as he said, As I have sworn in my wrath,
If they shall enter into my rest: "
Hebrews 4:3

* In Adam, we were condemned to judgement. In Christ, we are justified.

"Therefore, as by the offence of one
judgement came upon all men to condemnation;
even so by the righteousness of one
the free gift came upon all
men unto justification of life"
Romans 5:18

"He that believeth on the Son hath
everlasting life: and he that believeth
not the Son shall not see life;
but the wrath of God abideth on him"
John 3:36

* Adam was formed of the earth earthly. Jesus Christ is the messiah from heaven. No man went to heaven before the advent of Jesus.

"Jesus said unto them, If God were your Father,
ye would love me: for I proceedeth
forth and came from God: neither
came I of myself, but he sent me"
John 8:42

Conclusion   The Revelation of Restoration

✵   Adam received life from God whereas Christ is the life of God personified.

> *"He that hath the Son hath life;*
> *and he that hath not the*
> *Son of God hath not life"*
> *1 John 5:12*

> *"And so it is written, The first man Adam*
> *was made a living soul; the last Adam was*
> *made a quickening spirit".*
> *1 Corinthians. 15:45*

✵   Adam through disobedience and sin lost his great dominion and authority. Jesus Christ through his obedience shall forever retain and increase dominion.

> *"Of the increase of his government and peace*
> *there shall be no end, upon the throne of David,*
> *and upon his kingdom, to order it and to establish it*
> *with judgement and with justice from henceforth*
> *even for ever ..." Isaiah 9:7*

Job was born into Adam so he did not have a choice. Today, the case is different; we have an option to be in the first of the second Adam. You can decide to let Christ be risen in you. God has made it possible for you to come in contact with this book. Job did not have a messiah, he served God. No blood was shed for him, but he repented before the Lord and got his restoration.

Conclusion

It is your turn to rise up, embrace the gospel of Jesus Christ and possess your restoration. It is God that wants you restored. There is no limit for your life. God has designed the world to put you in charge. Rise up!

*Remember, you must be born again.
If you must farewell in the scene
You must say farewell to sin
if you have submitted your life to the
Lordship and Messiahship of Jesus Christ,
I shall be delighted to receive your
mail or your call soonest.
You can write:*

DR. BEN ATTAH
*e-mail: benattah@excite.com
or call*
☎: *01-7737261, 0802-640-2441*
REVELATION PUBLISHERS
P. M. B. 0142 Festac Town, Lagos

*May the Lord bless and keep you in
Jesus precious name! Amen.*

The Revelation of Restoration

The Revelation of Restoration

www.ingramcontent.com/pod-product-compliance
Lightning Source LLC
LaVergne TN
LVHW020442070526
838199LV00063B/4821